STO

ACPL ITEM
DISCARDED

S0-BWT-617

12.95 A

1-16-75

THE BARONS OF EUROPEAN INDUSTRY

The Barons of European Industry

EDITED BY ANTHONY ROWLEY

HOLMES AND MEIER PUBLISHERS, INC
New York

Published in the United States of America 1974
by Holmes & Meier Publishers, Inc.
101 Fifth Avenue, New York, NY 10003

© 1974 by Anthony Rowley
All right reserved

Library of Congress Cataloging in Publication Data

Rowley, Anthony.
    The Barons of European Industry.

    Bibliography: p.
    1. Big business–European Economic Community
countries.–Addresses, essays, lectures. 2.   Corporations–European Economic Community countries.–
Addresses, essays, lectures. 3. Capitalists and financiers
–European Economic Community countries–Addresses,
essays, lectures. I. Title.
HD2844.5.R69   338.6'44'094   74-11193

ISBN 0–8419–0171–6

Printed in Great Britain

1848876

CONTENTS

CHAPTER 1   THE DOMAINS OF EUROPEAN INDUSTRY

Anthony Rowley

Much has been written about the march of the great U.S. multinational corporations across post-war Europe, about the supposedly inexorable advance of the IBMs, General Motors, ITTs and Du Ponts of this world. Indeed so much has been said about the way these leviathans are coming to rival nations in their power and wealth that it might excusably be supposed they already have a stranglehold on the economies of Europe, or soon will have. One might also suppose that they dominate the most important sectors of European industry, or will come to do so in time. However, the impact of the multinationals has often been exaggerated.* They have scarcely penetrated many of the vital sectors of European industry; moreover there is good reason for thinking that the great American business adventure in Europe is losing momentum and that the future will be a period of consolidation rather than advance. Jean-Jacques Servan Schreiber's *defi americain* already seems rather a hollow challenge.

Yet if the names of many U.S. multinationals are now household words in Europe, the same can hardly be said of the great European national companies that are still really at the heart of Continental industry, nor of the powerful interests which control them. Names such as Krupp, Philips, Renault, Fiat and British Leyland admittedly spring readily to mind in the context of European industry. But how many people are so readily familiar with, say, Thyssen, the German steel giant and with the vastly wealthy Thyssen family and foundation who still own a large part of it, or with the powerful 'Quandt' and 'Flick' interests in Germany who control Mercedes-Benz and BMW? Who knows what has happened to Krupps nowadays? How many people who know of, or even own, Fiat cars know also that the Fiat empire in Italy is virtually an industrial state in itself, or are familiar with the name of the wealthy and aristocratic Agnelli family which runs it?

For that matter it is doubtful whether many people outside France

---

*'When the foreign subsidiaries (of U.S. multinationals) are considered in the context of the countries where they operate, their relative dimensions shrink and they ordinarily account for a small share of the total manufacturing product – perhaps 6 per cent in Western Europe.' Robbins & Stobaugh.[1]

or even within it know much about Michelin beyond the fact that it makes radial tyres. This is hardly surprising considering the lengths to which the secretive and autocratic Michelin family will go in order to avoid publicity. Yet even their secrecy is almost as nothing compared to that of the Brenninkmeyer family which controls the C & A concern in Holland -- and indeed of most of the Dutch big business concerns. Nor are Michelin's links with Citroën (and formerly with Fiat in Italy) well known. Again, these hidden links, fascinating though they are, pale into relative insignificance alongside the multiple holdings of the Boël, Janssen and Solvay families in Belgium and of the mighty Société Générale. The Baron Lambert is another power figure in Belgian industry, yet his name and interests are as little known to most people as are those of the legendary French textile magnate, Marcel Boussac, or of Marcel Dassault, one of the most remarkable figures in industry anywhere as well as in France. It is hardly likely that those who are unfamiliar with what the de Rothschilds control in France will even have heard of Arnold Maersk McKinney Møller, head of the Maersk industrial empire in Denmark and the biggest shipowner in Europe. Who knows much of Irish industry beyond the name 'Guinness', which is no longer an Irish company anyway, and what of the true power figures in British industry. Are they the new managerial barons like Lord Stokes of British Leyland or the lineal barons like Lord Pilkington, head of the international glassmaking concern. Or are men like Jim Slater of Slater Walker, as has been said, the true 'power brokers in a modern society'.

If the United States is the home of the great multinational business corporation then Europe is essentially the home of the great family business dynasties still, surpassed only by Japan perhaps in this respect. European industry is not dominated solely by family interests however. There are the renowned (or some might say, notorious) holding companies -- *les holdings* -- of which the most remarkable must be the Société Générale de Belgique in Belgium whose tentacles spread into just about every corner of the country's industry and commerce. There are the equally ubiquitous and omnipotent para-statal corporations in Italy, such as IRI and ENI. Founded in 1933 under Mussolini, IRI is now the major shareholder in such diverse groups as Alitalia, Alfa Romeo and in shipbuilding, steel, engineering, cement production and banking. IRI was set up to rescue three Italian banks from bankruptcy and thus came by its powerful portfolio of industrial shares almost by accident through this method of backdoor nationalisation. In the Republic of Ireland the Government also has a strong vested interest in industry via the Irish Life insurance company. Denmark has at least one holding company too, in the shape of the powerful East Asiatic Company.

In Germany the power of the big banks is almost legendary and though their influence in industry is sometimes exaggerated it is nevertheless remarkable by other countries' standards. The Deutsche Bank for instance owns more than 25 per cent of Daimler-Benz and a like proportion of Karstadt, one of the country's leading department store chains, in which the Commerzbank has a similar stake. Commerz and Dresdner banks have equally big shares in Kaufhof, another department store chain, while Dresdner owns a quarter of Metallgesellschaft, the metals concern, and Bayern-Hypo bank in Bavaria has become known as the brewery bank because of the stakes it holds in that important sector. In France the Banque de Paris et des Pays Bas, one of the so-called *Banque d'affaires* and one of the few big French banks which is not state owned, has very extensive industrial and financial interests, as do some of the state banking groups such as the Banque National de Paris. The public institution, Caisse des Dépôts et Consignations is a powerful vehicle for industry finance. In Britain there is talk of the clearing banks taking a more active rôle in industry ownership -- a rôle they have shunned so far. At present the so-called financial institutions, insurance companies, pension funds and invest-ment trusts play the chief financing role in British industry albeit a very passive one.

What of the rôle of the state in European industry, nowhere more pronounced than in Italy. In Britain the Post Office, railways, coal mining, steel, electricity and gas generation are among the state controlled undertakings and, though many of these functions are common to state operations elsewhere in Europe, the pattern is by no means uniform. In Germany, electric power is largely in private hands, as is part of the coal-mining industry as well, of course, as steel. Yet the country's biggest automobile manufacturer, Volkswagen, is part owned by the state. Likewise, Renault in Paris has been effectively owned by the French Government since the war. In Italy much is nominally owned by the state via IRI. In Ireland the state controls most public transport and -- a nicely Irish touch -- the exploitation of the peat bogs.

What, finally, of Europe's very own, multinational companies, so beloved by the architects of the EEC? They talked a great deal of fostering bigness in industry to beat off the American challenge, hardly realising that this very concept would be challenged with time and that the *défi americain* would recede. The number of cross-frontier mergers or proposed mergers in Europe can be counted on the fingers of one hand – Agfa-Gevaert, Dunlop Pirelli, Rheinstahl and Thyssen, Hoogovens-Hoesch and Rothmans International – and they have hardly been a conspicuous success to date. Neither have many of the national mergers which came about in the rush to industrial concentration during the 1960s.

In short, the industrial landscape presents very different pictures from one part of the EEC to another. The growth of the U.S. multinationals and of indigenous multinationals has done little to impose uniformity upon it, no more than have the efforts of the Brussels eurocrats for all their incessant talk of 'harmonisation'.

It is on industry in the nine countries that make up the Europe of the Common Market that this book concentrates. It is a sketch of some of the more colourful sections in what is an intricate patchwork, and a portrait of some of the more prominent personalities involved. It explodes one or two myths, such as the view of France as an inefficient agricultural nation overshadowed by Germany's industrial might. On the contrary, the German economic miracle seems to be giving way to a French miracle now. Professionalism is an equal force with paternalism in modern-day France. All is not chaos in Italy, though conditions may sometimes verge upon it. Germany's old industrial order from pre-war days has not disappeared despite the post-war reconstruction of the economy. Belgium does fit its traditional image, however, in the sense that it remains in the grip of the holding companies, while Luxembourg remains the legendary tax haven for foreign business. Holland has derived considerable industrial strength from the EEC and Denmark, is no longer the agricultural state it once was. Ireland too prospers within the EEC, though that prosperity is in part mortgaged to foreigners. Meanwhile the roots of Britain's industrial troubles probably go back to the industrial revolution. There is no such thing as 'European' industry – there is French industry, German industry, British industry and so on. Vive la différence.

CHAPTER 2   FRANCE: THE MASK OF MODERNITY

Rupert Cornwell

'Chère vieille France! La bonne cuisine! Des Folies Bergères! Le gai Paris! La haute couture et de bonnes exportations: du cognac, du champagne, des Bordeaux ou du Bourgogne! C'est terminé. La France a commencé et largement entamé une révolution industrielle . . . ' (President Pompidou's Press Conference of 21 September 1972.)

The autocratic old president of one of France's myriad family companies had decided it was the moment for a change. 'Gentlemen,' he told the assembled board one day, 'the time has come for new blood. I propose to set the example myself by bringing in a talented and dynamic young man. One day he will take over the business from me. Let me introduce him to you.' The door then opened to reveal a shy and nervous young man, who just managed to stammer 'Thank you, Daddy.'

This sort of joke about the state of French industry is heard less often today. Once an economic laughing stock in Europe, France has staged a miraculous recovery in the last fifteen years. No European country has sustained a faster rate of economic growth, and the euphoric forecasts of the Hudson Institute suggest that by 1985 the country will be the biggest economic power in Europe. Last year France was the third biggest exporter in the world, ahead of both Japan and Britain. More significantly, she is losing her image of a supplier of primarily agricultural goods. In 1972 finished products accounted for over 50 per cent of French exports, against only 46 per cent five years before. Many would ascribe this economic renaissance to the success of the state's *dirigiste* management of the nation's affairs over the last fifteen years, but it is as much due to the stark fact that France in 1958, on the eve of accession to the fledgling Common Market, was faced with a sink-or-swim choice. Against the advice of a number of leading economists General de Gaulle devalued the franc, and gave French industry the necessary competitive edge it needed to compete with Germany. Since then the economy has not looked back.

President Pompidou saw his most important task as consolidating this early success and completing the transformation of France into a major economic power. In general he curbed French ambitions, trying

5

to keep them within a realistic framework. Whereas the General will be remembered for prestige projects such as the Concorde and the nuclear 'force de frappe', his successor left his imprint in more prosaic ventures; the impressive new airport that opened in March 1974 at Roissy-en-France and the vast new congress hall at the Porte Maillot on the western fringe of Paris, inaugurated a month earlier. Unlike Concorde, neither stands on the forefront of technology, but both are the hallmark of the prosperous, transformed France.

There is no more striking instance of this change than the decline of the small family firm. It is true that the boards of many of France's largest companies are sprinkled with the names of the original family, but a closer look shows that their positions are often honorific. The real 'chief-executives' are the new race of managers and entrepreneurs, often boasting degrees obtained at U.S. business schools.

There were several reasons for this change. There was the war, and the embarrassing rôles that the families sometimes found it impossible to explain in the fighting's bitter aftermath. As the anecdote which opened the chapter illustrates, suitable heirs simply could not always be found. Heavy death duties were another factor, while the investments required to keep abreast of the competition from the U.S.A., Japan and Europe called for sums which could not be met from the pockets of a few individuals, however wealthy. The only alternative for many a proud family was to open up its shares to the public, and, of course, dilute its own control.

It would be equally wrong however to assume that this process is now complete, that a country famous for its small companies and smaller farmers has blossomed into the complete industrial state, bursting with multinational corporations. The trend is simply continuing, and in many sectors much too slowly for the liking of the Government. France is one of the most fundamentally conservative countries in Europe, and it is surprising that so much has been achieved with so little trauma. Today, the country still does not appear as high as it should in any league table of the biggest corporations. In a list of the top 1,000 companies in the Europe of the Nine, which appeared in the French business magazine *L'Entreprise*, there were only 165 French representatives, against 201 from West Germany and 254 from Britain — and this despite the fact that the French gross national product is now at least half as large again as that of the United Kingdom. In the narrower field of the top 50, the same nations achieve 10th, 17th, and 15th place respectively, and it is not until 19th place that the first French name occurs — the state-owned car group of

Renault.

The picture of France as a source of many of the more enjoyable things in life, rather than as a centre of big business, is hard to dispel. Two years ago President Pompidou felt obliged to bid an ironic farewell to the traditionally famous products of the country, such as paté de foie gras, champagne and fine cognac. Like the foods themselves, his remarks were largely for foreign consumption but they did serve to bring home a truth which is frequently overlooked; that the country's new richness is founded on exports of machine tools to West Germany, rather than of fine clarets to the English landed gentry. How quickly things are changing can be assessed after a quick glance at the list of France's top twenty-five companies. Essentially only the big three car companies — Peugeot and Citröen (now to merge) and Renault — and the major French oil company CFP have retained their position over the past decade. Among the others Rhône-Poulenc (chemicals) has been lifted up to its present fourth place by a series of large acquisitions, while the unwieldy names of Saint-Gobain-Pont-à-Mousson (chemicals, engineering) and Pechiney-Ugine-Kuhlmann (chemicals, metals) bear witness to the recent mergers that have lifted them to sixth and fifth place in the table respectively. In that top twenty-five it is only Peugeot which can probably claim to be a real 'family' company. Five Peugeots sit on the 11-man board, and the effective managing director of the group, Francois Gautier, has married into the clan. The company incidentally affords the lesson that old-fashioned formulae can still pay dividends; over the past few years Peugeot has been consistently the most successful of the French car companies. So much so that it seems likely to emerge as the dominant partner in the new Peugeot-Citroën merger.

It has indeed been a decade of upheavals and many of the participants are now happy to catch their breaths for a moment and consolidate their new positions. At the same time embedded in the structure of French industry and in many of its key sectors are still to be found the great family empires; some of them a little unsteady as their masters move into their 80s but still solidly supported by the paternalistic traditions that run so deep in France, and buttressed by the belief that private business is literally private with no need for outsiders (including journalists) to be kept informed.

Family Empires

None exemplifies the problems of today more perfectly than the Dassault-Breguet group, founded and still run by the near legendary Marcel Dassault, one of the most remarkable figures in industry anywhere. Dassault, now a rather fragile but still acutely intelligent 82-year-old, has been a Gaullist deputy since 1958 and holds undisputed sway over his seat at Beauvais, a cathedral town some fifty miles north of Paris. His main claim to fame is the brilliant Mirage family of jets, whose design and construction has been jealously supervised by Marcel Dassault himself. The Mirage is the biggest export earner ever to come out of a French aircraft factory, and some 1,200 have now been sold abroad. Their popularity among Arab oil sheiks is now famous. In 1967, Avions Marcel Dassault bought out the smaller Breguet Aviation, and the group is now quoted on the Paris Bourse.

But now his golden touch seems to have deserted him; for the short haul Mercure, on which Dassault had built his hopes for capturing a large part of the world civilian market, is proving to be a very costly failure. In February the Government publicly washed its hands of the project. The exact financial state of the Dassault empire is still uncertain but if the Government is forced to intervene, it will certainly mean loss of independence, and there are many officials who would welcome the opportunity to force the autocratic old man into line.

Curiously enough for all his imperiousness of manner and past success with his products, Dassault is still regarded as something of a *parvenu* by France's dwindling band of family magnates. The *doyen* of them all is probably the 84-year-old Marcel Boussac who presides in sad and lonely splendour over a crumbling textile empire in the north of France. Boussac in fact presents a perfect example of the problems of over-concentrated power. Part of his problem, certainly, is the general condition prevailing in the textile industry itself which has fallen on bad times everywhere in Europe. But despite over 55 years in the business, Boussac has not seemed ready or able to make the changes needed to survive. Cash crisis followed cash crisis, and in 1971 came the unedifying spectacle of a piecemeal sale of the perfume and fashion house Christian Dior, which he owned, to the dynamic Moët-Hennessy drinks group.

Boussac still rules his kingdom, and, whatever happens, he will die an enormously wealthy man. His personal fortune, which includes newspaper interests, property and racehorses, is rumoured to be worth some £40 million.

Here the lack of a natural successor is glaringly apparent, as on a successful outcome depends the future of some 16,000 jobs in the textile industry alone. Boussac's attitude of lofty independence has unfortunately alienated the Paris Industry Ministry, who might best have been able to help him. They have been quoted as saying, 'What can we do? From an industrial viewpoint other companies are more deserving of help — and besides, no outsider has ever gained a foothold with Boussac.' The only person who seems to have had much influence on him is a former governor of the Bank of France, Jacques Brunet, whose painstaking report and advice helped him through the difficult days of 1970 and 1971. But the fundamental problems still remain.

As has been said, his difficulties are partly those of the textile industy, which has been in decline. Its hard times are reflected in its down-at-heel and depressing towns, places like Roubaix and Tourcoing wedged near the Belgian border. Countless family concerns, less well buttressed than Boussac, were faced with the choice of rationalisation or death, and during this process some of the less acceptable faces of French capitalism have been brutally revealed.

In February 1974, a Paris court started to hear of the strange adventures of the Willot brothers, who took advantage of the prevailing economic situation to build up an empire of textile and property interests worth £200 million and employing 27,000 people. The 146 charges against them include tampering with balance sheets, payment with fraudulently inflated shares, and old-fashioned U.K.-style asset stripping. The outcome of the trial will show how far French company law has kept abreast of the changes in the country's industrial picture. Surrounded by a secrecy that is legendary, the family enterprise of the Michelin tyre company is flourishing as never before. The exact sales figures are impossible to gauge, but the best-informed guesses are of upwards of Frs 7,000 million a year world-wide. The French parent's annual report in its drab brown cover, reminiscent of an old civil service manual, is an eloquent enough statement of what the group feels about prying strangers. It gives little away and what it does is instantly nullified by the fact that nothing is consolidated and that its operations outside France are handled by a Swiss holding company, if anything even more taciturn than its French counterpart.

Michelin is the exception to every modern management recipe for success. It is based in the pleasant but isolated upland city of Clermont Ferrand in central France and it is run on the most antiquated paternalistic lines. The Anglo-Saxon style financial analyst would not be allowed within miles of the place. And yet the formula works, for almost alone among French companies Michelin has successfully competed against the American giants. The radial tyre, pioneered in Clermont Ferrand, and now being copied in Akron, Ohio was the foundation of this success. One French bank has estimated that radial tyres might account for no less than 90 per cent of the world's new tyre market. This may be a little exaggerated, but the potential for Michelin is clear enough.

The company is renowned for its secrecy. Michelin men are encouraged not to mix with outsiders, and enquirers are turned away. Even General de Gaulle, in the heat of the triumph of the Liberation, was allowed no further than into the outer courtyard of the company's works at Clermont-Ferrand. The ruling family is led by François Michelin who is the 47-year-old grandson of Edouard Michelin the founder of the empire. He has spent his whole life with the company. Directly under him are 25,000 men, one eighth of the entire population of Clermont-Ferrand.

It is less often remarked that Michelin is the head of one of the largest industrial groups in Europe. Michelin holds a controlling interest in France's third largest car-maker, Citroën, whose public relations bears all the hallmarks of Michelin breeding. The company also effectively controls its smaller French rival, Kleber-Colombes. Apart from the Flick family in Germany, there can be few dynasties in Europe with such a large say in key sectors of the economy of any one country.

But in France as anywhere else the Michelins are the exception. The companies of the big families become quoted on the Bourse, and circumstances force other changes in turn on the companies concerned. Henri De Wendel, the steel baron, is one such. His fame was once almost synonymous with the whole steel-producing region of eastern France, but it has now followed the area itself into something of a decline. The huge investments required in steel manufacture forced him long ago to open up ownership of his company, and now another equally radical transformation is taking place with the large-scale migration of the industry away from the cold harsh landscapes of Lorraine to Fos on the Mediterranean. 12,500 jobs will disappear over the next few years, but the French steel industry should emerge in a healthier state than most of its European competitors.

Efficient, Grey Corporations

Since 1945, the old families have given way to the efficient grey corporation. In the last five years their hold on the economy has in fact increased dramatically, largely as a result of the Government's eager and successful efforts to restructure the key areas of industry. This was already taking place in the latter years of de Gaulle's rule in the 1960s but blossomed fully with President Pompidou, who subordinated national grandeur to national prosperity in a way his predecessor never did. Metals, electronics and chemicals are just a few of the industries to have been overhauled, and out of the mergers have grown such world famous and giant-sized companies as Pechiney Ugine Kuhlmann (PUK), Saint-Gobain-Pont-à-Mousson, and Rhône-Poulenc. The big groups have tidied up their overlapping and irrelevant interests, with corresponding gains to both their efficiency and profitability. Their shares are widely spread throughout the public, with the biggest single interest often - as in the case of Saint-Gobain and the Cie Financière de Suez — being held by a *banque d'affaires*.

Many of the once despised Anglo-Saxon habits have crept into their style. Words like 'le cashflow', 'le marketing', and 'l'engineering' pepper the conversation of their executives, and financial analysts are treated with respect. Accounts are dutifully consolidated in the best Price Waterhouse tradition, and the bravest are even venturing to such foreign fields as the London Stock Exchange. Their drive for efficiency has inevitably bred soullessness in many cases, frequently leaving them without public identity, outside the graphs of the chartists and financial analysts. One reason, of course, is the lack of advertising by French companies in comparison with their Anglo-Saxon counterparts. A case in point is Rhône-Poulenc, France's flagbearer in the world chemical industry. Despite its size it is little known outside France and curiously ignored by the public within. Some improvement came with a well-conceived advertising campaign to establish in people's minds, that the company was present everywhere in national life, followed by the introduction of a futuristic company emblem based on the letters RP: but it is still firmly in the shadows of its three German rivals, Hoechst, Bayer and BASF, not to mention ICI and the American giants like Du Pont.

Signs are appearing however that this particular slumbering colossus is about to awake. M. Wilfrid Baumgartner, a former Finance Minister under de Gaulle, presided over an era of rapid expansion studded with mergers and absorptions. But he gave the impression of a

lofty father figure instead of a committed industrialist, and last summer
he was replaced by Renaud Gillet; and it is he who will have the
formidable task of turning Rhône–Poulenc into an outward looking
entity for the 1980s and 1990s.

In a sense his is a family appointment. His grandfather was partly
responsible for the birth of the tiny Lyons company that has now
emerged as an empire employing over 130,000 people and which is
France's largest private company in terms of assets. Gillet himself is a
Lyonnais, and was a boy of 15 when Usines de Rhône and
Établissements Poulenc Fréres merged to give Rhône-Poulenc its name.
Today at sixty there is little obvious in his past to suggest that he is the
right man to give the group an international stature commensurate with
its size.

On casual inspection Gillet does not seem the most suitable of
candidates, but appearances are deceptive. He is an animated man, and
unlike his predecessor actually gives the impression that he enjoys
talking about Rhône-Poulenc, even its problems. In the few months
that he has controlled the £1,300 million-a-year concern, he has
initiated a sweeping overhaul of the management structure. 'The time
of big acquisitions is over.' he says after the frenetic expansion of the
late 1960s and early 1970s. The broad spread of Rhône-Poulenc's
activities, from petrochemicals to pharmaceuticals, has been reorganised
into separate product divisions each headed by a new executive
committee. Not the least important, there is a more friendly
atmosphere at the group's staid headquarters at the Avenue Montaigne
in Paris. Only in the U.S., where lack of self-confidence has held back
Rhône-Poulenc and many other French companies, will a deliberate
expansion policy be pursued. 'America,' he admits frankly, 'is our
biggest weakness.' Gillet's comparative youth will undoubtedly be one
of his biggest assets. In keeping with many others the board of
Rhône-Poulenc has often seemed like an elderly and well-connected
Lyonnaise club. He is the second youngest on the 12-man board, which
includes a career diplomat and an eminent doctor. Seven of them are
already over seventy; of the others, men like Pierre Jouven of the
newly-merged metals group Pechiney Ugine Kuhlmann, are too busy to
contribute much more than an occasional, if prestigious, expertise to
the affairs of Rhône-Poulenc. Everything will depend on the younger
managers that Gillet has brought in at the level just below the top.

Rhône-Poulenc's problems are a good illustration of what French
industry as a whole is facing. It has only recently woken up to the fact
that publicity can be a good thing, and that the secrecy of the past has

been a root cause of the depression of the Paris Bourse. In order not to spread the equity base and allow partial ownership outside the charmed inner circle, a French chairman will always prefer to raise new money by bond issues rather than share issues. In fact the system has worked well financially and vast sums of money are raised each year in this way; but the very popularity of it condemns the Bourse to obscurity. When he was at Rhône-Poulenc, M. Baumgartner did head a prestigeous Commission to report on how to revive the share market. Many of his recommendations were, and are, being adopted by the Government, but the market is still in the doldrums, and a contested take-over bid is very rare. The Saint-Gobain affair was one exception to this, in the winter of 1968/69. This take-over struggle was uniquely educative in the circumstances that led up to it, the passions it aroused at the time, and in the changes it forced on the French public's view of industry, as well as within industry itself.

It is as well to start with the protagonists in the drama. In the autumn of 1968, Antoine Riboud had already emerged as one of the most driving forces in the French business world. He headed the glass concern BSN, which had grown under his guidance from an old fashioned Lyons-based concern, Souchon-Neuvesel, into a threatening, if much smaller, rival to the giant of the industry, the venerable and sprawling Saint-Gobain. His ideas were innovative – as well they might be in a man whose brothers were Jean Riboud, head of the New York based oil services group Schlumberger, and Marc, the world famous news photographer.

Riboud had grasped that Saint-Gobain was in a precarious situation: its aristocratic president Arnaud de Vogüe had allowed the company which had found fame in the days of Louis XIV, to slide financially. Technologically too, BSN was far ahead. Riboud offered a merger of the two companies, but Saint-Gobian refused, even though the proposal had the tacit blessing of the Government. Then came the move that electrified financial Paris: BSN put in a £70 million bid for its rival, and included in the offer a precedent-setting convertible bond option. This was so strange that it in fact proved to be an element in the bid's ultimate failure. At first, it seemed as if the BSN assault would succeed. Saint-Gobain was forced to open to the public gaze what had been one of the most reticent of companies. Attractive offers rained on the shareholders, to persuade them not to accept the offer. Some supporters carried the struggle further and threw bombs into the BSN headquarters near the Madeleine.

Imperceptibly at first, the tide started to change. The convertible bond was a strange animal to the stolid French investors. More significantly, unidentified buying started to drive the Saint-Gobain shares up. As the offer drew to a close, brokers were sent into the market with unlimited buy orders for Saint-Gobain. Finally Riboud admitted failure but the mystery over the unknown ally of Saint-Gobain persisted; wild stories circulated about Europe's business aristocracy stepping in to support a relative in distress, and companies in Switzerland, Belgium and even Britain were forced to deny that they had conspired to thwart BSN.

Six months later the mystery was cleared up, but the victory of Saint-Gobain proved to be Pyrrhic. The ally was one of the big two Paris *banques d'affaires*, the Cie Financiére de Suez; and the price of its friendship was a shotgun marriage for Saint-Gobain with the unglamorous but well-run construction and engineering concern of Pont-à-Mousson. The President of the new group was a professional manager, Roger Martin of Pont-à-Mousson, and Suez turned out to be its largest shareholder. Almost everyone involved in this affair has prospered. Saint-Gobain-Pont-à-Mousson has grown into one of France's most successful companies, to the delight of the financial analysts. Profits have been rising at something like 20 per cent per annum, the debt structure has been vastly improved, and as the final feather in its cap, it has recently acquired a London Stock Exchange listing.

M. Riboud was undeterred by his failure. BSN quickly launched a major expansion programme and gained control of the Evian mineral water and Kronenbourg brewery groups. At the end of 1972 came the crowning stroke, a merger with the foods group Gervais-Danone, of yoghourt and cream cheese fame, to create a £800 million-a-year conglomerate which is Europe's fourth largest manufacturer of foodstuffs. M. Riboud is renowned for his imaginativeness in labour relations, not the traditional strong point of French employers; but this is matched by a managerial toughness that has earned him a reputation for authoritarianism. He relishes his image as one of France's less conventional business leaders.

The other lesson that was handed out to the French public by the BSN Saint-Gobain battle was the enormous power wielded by the *banque d'affaires*. They are best compared to the London merchant banks, except that they take involvement with industry one step further and often actively run immense holdings in various sectors. Suez, and its arch rival Paribas (Banque de Paris et des Pays Bas) dominate the field, although they are far from alone.

Of the two, Paribas is probably stronger abroad and Suez stronger within France. Recent deals have strengthened this belief – the ambitious though widely criticised share exchange agreement between Paribas and Warburgs of London, and Suez' effective take-over of one of its closest rivals in France, the Banque de l'Indochine. Both of them have huge empires; and can, as in the case of Paribas and the paper industry, re-organise entire sectors of business by the redeployment of their holdings. The decision of the French Government in 1966 to abolish the distinction between deposit and investment banks only increased their scope by making available even greater resources. Suez has recently stretched, through its property subsidiary La Henin, into the wine growing business – a far cry from its still heavy involvement with Saint-Gobain-Pont-à-Pousson.

Entrepreneurs

Banks are a frequent figure head for private groups – none more so than the legendary Rothschilds. The richest is probably Edmond who is the least known of them. He has used his own vehicle Cie Financière to back such disparate and unlikely ventures as holiday resorts and pipelines. The three financiers are Guy, Alain and Elie, and their bank even threw itself open to deposits from the public before cooling down on the idea.

Curiously the importance of the French Rothschilds lies not in their famous banking activities – they do not rank high in the international bank business – but in industry, and more specifically the unglamorous mining industry.

Guy de Rothschild is the president of Le Nickel Penarroya. It is France's most important mining group, and owns some of the world's most fabulous nickel deposits in the overseas territory of New Caledonia in the Pacific. In a touching gesture of modernity, a few years ago the company moved its head offices out of the elegant eighteenth-century Place Vendôme to the shiny and most un-Rothschild-like brashness of the Tour Montparnasse, the 600-foot skyscraper on Paris' Left Bank.

The move did their business fortunes little good, for the world nickel market entered a slump that saw Le Nickel suffer a Frs 80 million loss in 1972, and despite a late recovery of prices, 1973 saw a further loss of Frs 72m.

The relevance of the Rothschilds to modern France lies mostly in the £400 million minerals empire that they control, and not in banking where their scope and resources inevitably do not measure up to the distinction of the name.

The public has been allowed to buy shares in both Le Nickel and Compagnie du Nord, the holding company at the apex of the Rothschilds' empire, but not even the honour of owning stock in the same business as a Rothschild can compensate for the hard times on which the company has fallen. Still, it was perhaps some consolation to hear Baron Guy smoothly explaining all away at the annual general meeting earlier this year, and suavely hinting at the presence of enormous cash reserves which will support the company should the situation not improve. This cursory review of the private sector inevitably leaves too many people and empires unmentioned. There is the young Belgian industrialist Baron Edouard Empain, who is based in Paris and controls through the Schneider financial group some of the key strategic points of the steel, electronics and nuclear industries – not always to the pleasure of the Government, which aims to keep such important matters in the hands of thoroughbred Frenchmen.

Then there is Empain's frequent negotiating partner, the £1,000 million Compagnie Générale d'Électricité which has climbed back to the forefront of the heavy electrical industry through the efforts of its President Ambroise Roux. Next must come CGE's erstwhile accomplice and new rival Thomson-Brandt, which has emerged as the leading group in the household appliance sector, and has just decided to attack CGE's cosy position as one of the privileged suppliers to the French PTT (Post Office).

Nor are France's go-it-alone tycoons all ageing: a younger breed has emerged, either overhauling traditional and inefficient French activities, like Jacques Borel in the food industry, or taking advantage of one of the great booms engendered by the age of affluence like Laurent Boix-Vives and his company Skis Rossignol. Borel is a boundlessly energetic brash ex-IBM man who decided that his vocation was to teach the French the delights of mass catering. He has succeeded, with the alliance of the W.R. Grace group of America and his garish restaurants are to be seen on every new motorway in France. Borel is easy to dislike. He is at times a parody of himself as the dynamic manager, not bothering to conceal his scorn for the old-fashioned private way of doing business that is still so common in France. For him it is cost effectiveness analyses and competence on the job that count, and he has the reputation of treating any shoddy work ferociously. Financially his record speaks for itself, as the French, so fond of their food, take to his fare with relish. Profits in 1973 were up some 38 per cent and the number of meals served climbed by only a little less.

Marcel Fournier's Carrefour supermarket chain has been to French shopping what Borel has been to French food. The formula has been similar, a successful attempt to link quality with volume. As a backhanded compliment the ever-powerful French small shop-keepers lobby drove a Bill through Parliament last autumn that will effectively limit the spread of supermarkets and hypermarkets in the country. This has pleased France's estimated one million small tradesmen, but as Fournier points out housewives will not appreciate the restrictions on competition and lower prices to which the National Assembly decision will lead.

The third in this random triumvirate of young business leaders is Laurent Boix-Vives who, like his company, comes from the rapidly expanding Alpine region of the Val d'Isere. Rossignol is the fastest growing ski equipment company in the world, and like Carrefour, it is one of the few glamour stocks on the staid Paris Bourse.

Boix-Vives has also had the courage and the foresight to enter the lion's den of the U.S. market which is so little tapped by French industrialists. This year he started up his own North American manufacturing plant, and is fully aware of the good reputation and chic that French brandnames have in many parts of the world. To its credit the Government in Paris recognised his gifts and in July 1973 named him as the new head of the Institut de Développement Industriel (IDI) which it set up to help the growth of small companies which needed capital.

The Mask of Modernity

Though this portrait gallery of the private sector of industry is incomplete and inevitably selective, nevertheless a fairly clear picture of the whole emerges. Its basic element is a drive towards modernity that in the space of the twenty-eight years since the end of the war has lifted France to the forefront of the European economy. Much of course is due to the Common Market and the extra markets it offered – perhaps the greatest debt that France owes to General de Gaulle, that he had the foresight to recognise this, for all the war he later declared on Brussels. An extra help has been the rigorously 'selfish' approach of successive Governments. Perhaps at times they have not played the international game by the rules, but they have steadfastly put French interests in first place. Often protected and consistently favoured at the expense of their foreign competitors, it has been a golden era for industry. Nevertheless, conditions in whole areas of French business are much as they were fifty years ago. Behind the glittering technological triumph of the Concorde and the insolent innovation of Citroën motorcars the backward and fragmented structure of many parts of industry still survives unharmed. The small shopkeepers are only a symbol of it. The food industry and the textile sector are only two of the examples of areas where predators from Britain and elsewhere can easily gain an important foothold.

A parallel case is the Paris Bourse, which, despite the efforts of modernisation of M. Baumgartner and others, is still relatively under-developed. Most of what is really important in French finance is played out in theatres other than the stock market: and its longstanding and not entirely unjustified reputation for crookedness is scarcely a help. To those like the Willot brothers who have recognised them, its unique characteristics can be a definite advantage. The brothers' most notorious *coup*, which is still recounted by Paris dealers, was the transaction which gave them control of the elderly and prestigious store Bon Marché. The four brothers offered the then president of Bon Marché five times the ruling share price to part company with his holding. Needless to say this extremely profitable operation was not extended to the ordinary shareholder. There is now an open distrust felt by the would-be investor which may not be allayed by a new take-over code protecting minority shareholders or by the fact that the Willots received suspended prison sentences of up to 18 months and fines of up to Frs 100,000. This sort of suspicious climate will hardly make shareholders part with their money. Logic has therefore dictated that another channel be used -- the long term debenture issue. This suits both parties admirably. The shareholder can be certain that he will receive a regular and encouragingly high annual yield (bonds now carry annual interest of almost 10 per cent spiced with generous tax concessions) and the company can be certain that it will not see a sizeablepart of its equity pass into possibly hostile hands.

Curiously, despite all the pressure to streamline the share market, the Government has accepted this state of affairs quite happily, and indeed, through the state enterprises, is the biggest single user of the bond market. Issues by private companies (such as Rhône-Poulenc or Michelin) of £40 million or £50 million are almost commonplace; while the state lending instututions like Crédit National, which supplies medium- and long-term funds to industry, and Crédit Agricole which does the same thing for farmers, often make issues of over £100 million a time. The strength of the domestic bond market has meant that French companies, even when they are allowed, have relatively slight recourse to the international capital market. One of its special advantages is that groups of smaller companies – in steels, chemicals, and electronics for example -- can band together and raise money in an offering -- with the added incentive, moreover that a bond offering is one-fifth the price of a share issue. It is thus on the backs of France's millions of small savers that the great post-war industrial revival has been carried. Their continual willingness to set aside up to 17 per cent of their income has allowed almost limitless sums to be tapped for financing industrial expansion. Hence the rôle of the bond market and the bombardment of dazzling savings brochures that confronts the would be depositor when he enters any French bank.

The corresponding weakness of French companies has been their lack of expertise in the market place. The product is invariably of a high quality, which has given a high reputation to goods with the label 'made in France' – but selling them is another matter. This explains the success of the unGallic approach of such people as Jacques Borel, and also that sneaking admiration which many Frenchmen harbour for the Americans, who certainly know about marketing.

Government in Industry

Any survey of the French industrial landscape would obviously be incomplete without examining the rôle of the Government, which is more powerfully felt in France than in any other West European country with the exception of Italy. In a sense it was the chaos wrought by the last war which forced the Government to intervene, but a taste for centralisation marked French officials long before 1945. In any case it is evident today that the Paris Government, in common with those of every other European country, is being called upon increasingly for help in high technology and high expense industries. Long before public money was required to endow the country with a viable computer industry and allow the hideously expensive Concorde programme to proceed, the state was already massively present in the oil industry, the motor industry and tobacco.

Perhaps the only sphere in which France is more orientated to the private sector is the steel industry – which in the past decade has rationalised itself into the two groups of Wendel-Sidelor and Usinor.

It would be unfair to say that everyone in these enterprises suffers from the traditional bureaucratic drabness. Many businessmen, nominally part of the Government machine, have carved out attractive niches for themselves. There is the ebullient and energetic Henri Ziegler at the financially troubled Aerospatiale, who was until very recently in charge of the French manufacturing end of Concorde and the most ardent salesman of the supersonic aircraft on either side of the Channel. Ziegler now has been superseded by the more reserved Charles Christofini — no less a European in his outlook over aerospace but perhaps a better man with figures and balance sheets than his predecessor. Ziegler, like his rival Marcel Dassault, is of that very typical species of French industrialist, the inventor who does not look far beyond the intrinsic merits of his product. The motor industry is dominated by Renault which holds some 33 per cent of the domestic market, and which for many years has been France's largest single exporting group. Like Citroën, its main manufacturing plants are clustered on the western edge of Paris, at Boulogne-Billancourt around an island in the Seine. The appearance of the complex is forbidding to the visitor, and yet at Renault have been forged some of the more progressive industrial relations techniques to be found in the entire country.

The idea of equity participation by employees on the shop floor was first tried out at Renault on a large scale. Nonetheless such innovations have not given the company immunity from labour problems. There was a lengthy strike in April and May 1973 which cost it 60,000 vehicles or 4 per cent of a year's output. Renault officials shrug when you point out to them that the state-owned group is plagued by strikes to a far greater extent than either Citroën or Chrysler France — both of which are bastions of 'feudalism,' and riddled with in-house unions.

Part of the explanation, as is recognised by Renault's chief executive Pierre Dreyfus (a descendant of that other more celebrated Dreyfus of French history) lies in the unique position the company has in determining industry's social responsibility. Because it is geographically near the centre of political power disturbances at Billancourt frequently merge indissolubly with the causes of the political Left. If the difficulties of the motor manufacturers grow worse as a result of the oil crisis it is impossible to say what will happen at Renault — apart from the fact that it will be, as always, in the eye of the hurricane, be it industrial or political.

It is still too early to make predictions about the industry on the power front. A lot depends on the degree of success France achieves in securing its own oil supplies. And here another pillar of the Government sector enters the picture – the oil companies.

In France there are essentially two, the state-owned Elf-Erap (which controls a publicly-quoted subsidiary Aquitaine), and the better-known Cie Francaise des Pétroles (CFP), responsible for the Total brand name. The official interest in CFP is a minority 35 per cent, but now, as the Quai d'Orsay pursues its own long-term privileged agreements from its Arab friends, the rôle of the companies as a mere arm of Government policy is more apparent than ever. Elf admits this, but CFP looks back nostalgically at its pioneering past in Iraq and Persia and still finds it hard to accept. Its executives talk on occasions as if it were one of the 'seven sisters', the exclusive club of majors which dominates the world oil scene.

The oil companies clearly demonstrate the fashion in which the state has its way. One way is through that most French of 'old boy' networks, the Grandes Écoles, which in Britain can perhaps be broadly compared with Balliol or in the United States with the Harvard Business School. The intellectual *camaraderie* that persists between old *élèves* allows the choking red tape which accompanies the making of any decision to be cut. The process is also friendlier than it might otherwise be, while its ubiquity can be judged from the quickest of glances at the French Who's Who. This frequently-shared background also helps to explain the exceptionally high calibre of senior French civil servants, which, when allied to the traditional Gallic articulateness, rarely fails to impress the foreigner.

This ability can spill over into arrogance, and is one of the prime causes of the touchiness of the French Government about foreign takeovers. Another is the economic inferiority complex that is still felt towards the Americans and, incredibly, the British. France is still prepared to make an international incident to keep what it believes to be an important company in French hands: the phrase 'seeking a French solution' has become a cliché. No-one felt this more than General de Gaulle, and the perhaps apocryphal story is still to be heard of the icy 'come stai' greeting he gave to the Michelin President when he was summoned to the Elysée in 1968 to explain the agreement of the Michelins to sell to the Italian Fiat their Citroën car subsidiary. Needless to say the deal did not go through. The exception which can be said conveniently to prove the rule was the surprising decision in February 1974 to permit the German company Hoechst to take over France's £250 million pharmaceutical group Roussel Uclaf. Roussel was one of those family companies which had been built up by one man – in this case Jean-Claude Roussel. When he died in a helicopter crash in 1972, the death duties were so heavy that a sale of shares was the only way to raise the money, though not perhaps necessarily to the Germans.

In fact there are signs now that the Government is alarmed at the way family companies can be broken by taxation, and the Finance Ministry is said to be studying a system whereby death duties could be met by sales of shares to the Government. If such an option had been offered to Roussel's widow it might have given the state control of the concern and prevented it from falling into foreign hands. But, the French can be charming too, even to those dollar imperialists from across the Atlantic. Henry Ford II has more than once been to lunch at the Elysée and not merely because President Pompidou admired his excellent French; only two years ago his company agreed to build a gear box plant near Bordeaux and rumours still recur that Ford will install a full-scale assembly plant somewhere in France.

Ultimately it is this singlemindedness on the priority of industrial development which is the best guarantee of France's economic future, given a reasonable political stability.

Monetary policy, credit policy, exchange rate policy – all have been subordinated to the need to ensure a 5 per cent annual growth rate, though President Giscard will probably subjugate economic growth more to the 'quality of life'. It is true that in the new economic conditions created by the energy crisis, France cannot escape the effects of whatever slowdown takes place in the West. But it is equally true that the Government will have a good try, and it is the readiness of the state to enforce its will that is the single most striking factor of today's industrial France.

The French would never allow a 'City' in Paris to wield such power as in London, and never would they hesitate to clip its wings if they considered the national economic interest so demanded. This is why Paris will never become a financial centre to rival London. The French argue, that it is the wide margin afforded to the City that has been a prime factor in Britain never having broken free from the stop-go cycle and balance of payments crises. And who is to say they are wrong?

CHAPTER 3 WEST GERMANY: PEOPLE BEFORE PROFITS

Malcolm Rutherford

'It's what I call the third generation rule: the first generation builds up the company, the second maintains its position and the third gets into difficulties.' (A German industrialist.)

German industry is little more than three generations old and has been in and out of difficulties from the start. The Industrial Revolution in Germany came late; most of the firms whose names are known throughout the world were founded in the latter part of the nineteenth century – close to 1871, the year of unification. They flowered fast. The Mannesmann brothers, for example, began in 1890 the manufacture of seamless steel tubes by a process which is still used today. In 1897 their firm built the world's largest pipeline -- to the Caucasus. In 1870 the Siemens concern, which had quickly established subsidiaries in Britain and Russia, provided the first telegraph links between London and Calcutta. In the same year German steel production was a few hundred thousand tons. By 1900 it was seven million tons and by 1913 nineteen million tons – way ahead of Britain where the Industrial Revolution had begun. Then came the First World War and nemesis. Among others, the Siemens investments in Britain and Russia were lost -- a fact which has made the Germans cautious about foreign investment ever since.

Industry began again, and the years 1925–6 saw some of the most spectacular mergers ever recorded. Eight of the largest chemical companies joined together to form I. G. Farben which was to become the world's biggest exporter until it was overtaken by General Motors. Four of the leading steel groups came together in the same way to form the Vereinigte Stahlwerke, surpassed in size only by the US Steel Corporation. Two of the leading motor companies merged to form Daimler-Benz. The reasons given in all cases were the same: economic necessity and the need to get together and rationalise in the face of inflation and foreign competition. Size was the philosophy of the Weimar Republic just as much as of the Third Reich.

The mergers paid off. Only twenty-six out of sixty-four car producers survived the depression of 1929--32, but Daimler-Benz was among them. I. G. Farben flourished on exports which consistently accounted for more than 50 per cent of sales until 1933. Then the home market began to grow again. And the technical achievements continued too. In 1928 Siemens built its first telex machine to give Germany the first telex network in the world and by 1939 it was the world's leading electrical employer.

The results of the Second World War were even more traumatic than the First. To the destruction by the bombing was added the loss of territory. About 90 per cent of the plant of AEG-Telefunken, for example, was in the east and much the same went for Bayerische Motoren Werke (BMW) and a host of others. Siemens in Berlin had its plant ransacked by the Russians. A policy of dismantlement and deconcentration was pursued by the Western Allies and aimed especially at the steel and chemical giants.

The industry which arose again in the Federal Republic was in many respects similar to that of the earlier Germany. To be sure, the old trusts were broken up, but often only to re-emerge later in a form not very different and often under the same people. 'It was only natural,' said Dr Dieter Spethmann, now the head of Thyssen, 'that we should set about regaining the lost children.' The driving force in this movement was none other than Dr Hans Guenther Sohl who joined the board of the Vereinigte Stahlwerke at the age of thirty-five at the beginning of the war and two years later was its deputy chairman. The Allies split up the concentration and Dr Sohl was interned. In 1953 he appeared on the board of the newly-formed August Thyssen Huette and by a series of mergers built it up into the largest steel producer in Europe — bigger than the Vereinigte Stahlwerke had ever been. The lost children had been found without great difficulty.

Profit a Dirty Word

There are other similarities with the past. There is the same emphasis on capital goods and heavy dependence on exports. The big German industries are still chemicals, cars, electricals and engineering. The companies do not on the whole make big profits. The business magazine *Vision* showed in October 1973 that just over 100 of Europe's 500 largest firms were German — against nearly 170 from Britain and eighty from France. But there were only fourteen German firms among the hundred most profitable — against Britain's sixty-seven, and the most profitable company operating in the country was the German subsidiary of IBM. Even Siemens, which prides itself on profit-consciousness and was number seven in Europe according to turnover, ranked only 171st in the profitability table. AEG-Telefunken, the country's number two electrical concern and twenty-second in Europe's sales league, was 289th.

In recent years the poor profits have been generally blamed on rapidly rising wage costs which began with the wildcat strikes of Autumn 1969. But it seems that the weakness was always there. In part it stems from the old paternalism where firms went to extraordinary lengths to ensure their workers' well being. Germany is littered with company towns - BASF at Ludwigshafen, Volkswagen at Wolfsburg and, most famous of all, Krupp at Essen. The latter especially provided social benefits, including housing, way beyond the requirements of the law, even at times acting as marriage-broker.

The tradition persists today. The German executive who in public decries the inflation and high wage demands is in fact showing only one side of his character. Back at the firm, he is as likely as not to be granting new house agreements above those negotiated with the trade unions. One of the most articulate of them all — the multilingual Dr Joachim Zahn of Daimler-Benz — did just this in 1973. The engineering union, I. G. Metall, had agreed to a settlement of around 8.5 per cent at a time when the economic outlook was uncertain. The economy then turned up and Daimler-Benz quickly paid an additional increase. Other firms quietly followed suit; in those which did not there was trouble — until the increase became general. The explanation was, as always, to keep production going and to hold on to skilled labour. It is not surprising that the 1973 results were less high than had been originally forecast.

At times it seems that profit is a dirty word. At one of the regular press conferences in which German companies specialise, Herr Ebehard von Kuenheim, the young head of BMW, almost shocked journalists by declaring an aim of raising profits to 4 per cent of turnover. It has not yet been achieved and there has been scant sympathy for this failure. There was more sympathy for the old Alfried Krupp who refused to shut down his locomotive division on the grounds that his workers would have nothing to do, and indeed Krupp and other giants of the Ruhr, such as Rheinstahl, have gone through periods of making no profits at all. There was no question of closing them down and when Krupp ran into liquidity difficulties in 1966-7, even in the free market economy no-one thought it remarkable that the Government should come to its aid.

The Worker's Voice

The situation has its positive side, of course. The German worker's loyalty to the firm is partly a product of the post-war period when the people had little else to be loyal to, and it goes deeper than a sense of belonging. The chemical workers at Ludwigshafen, for example, have been known to accept lower wage settlements than in the rest of the country because they realised BASF was going through a bad time. And German legislation too is framed for the avoidance of conflict. Besides the small number of trade unions — ironically an inheritance from the British occupation — labour laws make maximum allowance for mediation and for cooling off periods so that strikes are usually, though not always, averted after the unions have shown their strength through a strike ballot. Conciliation is also abetted through those peculiarly German institutions — the *Betriebsverfassung*, *Mitbestimmung* and the two-tier board.

The *Betriebsverfassungsgesetz*, or Works Constitution Act, which went into effect in 1972 was one of the major reforms of Chancellor Willy Brandt's coalition government. It was important because it made mandatory what some of the larger German firms had been practising for years, namely consultation at shop-floor level. The Act made it illegal for any employer to deny the demand for a works council. A firm with between 50 and 150 employees must have five works councillors and the numbers rise according to the length of the payroll. The councils have the right to be informed about the economic situation of the company and to be consulted about hiring and firing, plans to transfer labour to other plants, proposed closures, welfare facilities, working conditions and so on. Any employee is entitled to an interview with the company personnel officer to ask about his own future prospects. The Act was opposed by industry — but that was with its public face. The statement by the personnel director of BASF was more realistic. 'It could work well,' he said, 'but if the workers want to be awkward, they could close us down at will.' Then he added: 'Actually, it's the sort of thing we've had at BASF all along, and so have a lot of others.' So far the workers have not closed down the plants.

Mitbestimmung stands for co-determination or, literally, 'having a say in'. Like the trade union structure, it too was an inheritance from the British occupation. The British insisted that the workers in the coal, iron and steel industries (*Montanindustrie*) must have parity with the shareholders in a number of decision-making areas. They did this through creating what are known as the two-tier boards. In each

company, according to Germany company law, there is a supervisory
board known as the *Aufsichtsrat*, generally abbreviated to *AR*, and an
executive board or *Vorstand*. The *AR* broadly represents the shareholders who in fact elect it, while the function of the *Vorstand* is to
manage the company. As the name suggests, the *AR* does the
supervision. To it must be reported company strategy, turnover,
profitability, liquidity and any important financial matters at least four
times a year. It has the powers to hire and fire the members of the
Vorstand and to set their remuneration. It has ultimate sanction over all
major investment decisions, the closure of plants and takeovers. The
law says that it *should* meet every quarter, and that it *must* meet every
half year.

The head of the *Vorstand* used to be known as the *Generaldirektor*
and had powers to impose his own way when there were disagreements
among his fellow members. The Western Allies left this law alone on the
grounds that its character was 'not essentially National Socialist' and it
was the Germans themselves who changed it in 1966, making the
chairman of the board simply *primus inter pares*. Now he must bow to
majority decisions and even Herr Franz Heinrich Ulrich, generally
thought of as the head of the Deutsche Bank, is properly described as
no more than Board Spokesman (*Sprecher des Vorstands*). As someone
said, it makes him sound like the public relations officer, which in a
way he is.

The business of the *Vorstand*, however, remains that of running the
company. The British enforced their *Mitbestimmung* by insisting that
on the *AR*s of the coal, iron and steel industries (which were the main
industries in the British zone) the workers and the shareholders must be
equally represented. The size of the *AR* must be a multiple of three and
a maximum of twenty-one. Normally there are ten labour representatives and ten elected by the shareholders, plus one independent
who must be approved by both sides. Sometimes it works in odd ways.
The old head of the Hoesch steel company, Dr Friedrich Harders,
claimed at a press conference that the proposed merger with the Dutch
concern of Hoogovens had been fully approved by both unions and
shareholders. He fell short of saying that the *AR* vote was unanimous.
It transpired that it had been 20—1 with the single 'no' cast by the
independent, the only man there whose function was to be objective.

In other industries labour representatives constituted one third of
the *AR*, but in early 1974 Herr Brandt's coalition government reached
an agreement to extend the parity principle everywhere. It differs from
the *Montanindustrie* model in that it provides for ten labour repre-

sentatives and ten from the shareholders, but makes no allowance for
an independent extra man. This literal application of parity is based on
the theory that it is in the mutual interest for both sides to agree, and
in the end they usually do. The net result of all these checks and
balances in labour and company law is that in theory at least all parties
concerned should be aware of what is going on. Perhaps behind them is
no more than the old German desire for order, which has now been
codified.

Accountable Executives

How does it work in practice? The answer seems to be that it depends
on the personalities involved. The average German chief executive tends
to be at his desk not much after eight in the morning and to leave not
much before eight in the evening. He will tend to be driven in a
Mercedes — not too fast because of the risk of accidents. He will eat in
the canteen — a low calorie meal to make him live longer. He will take
regular holidays usually at the same place — either walking in the Black
Forest, in a chalet in Switzerland, or perhaps in the South of France.
He will have conventional and not always very well-informed views on
inflation or the world monetary situation which he will not hesitate to
give when once or twice a year the company holds a press conference.
His life is very largely his work.

    Some spend practically all their working lives at a single firm — like
Paul Reusch at the engineering concern Gutehoffnungshuette (GHH)
who achieved the remarkable feat for a manager of seeing the
succession pass to his son Hermann. Evidently he had understood the
secret of a good relationship with the chief shareholders — in this case
the Haniel family. The GHH is in fact the oldest industrial firm in the
Ruhr and means 'Iron Works of Good Hope'. It was founded in 1808
by members of three families, the Jacobis, the Haniels and the
Huyssens, of whom the Haniels were the most prolific. By 1912 the
Millionaires' Yearbook contained sixteen Haniel entries. Most of them
soon lost the taste for running the business and turned it over to the
professionals, though to this day a Haniel still sits as chairman of the
AR representing several hundred family shareholders. They also
tolerated a certain eccentricity. A subsequent head of the *Vorstand*,
Dr Dietrich Wilhelm von Menges, had a wild hairy appearance, and used
to turn up rather later than 8 a.m. at the office and at times even went
home to lunch. The GHH *Vorstand* has only two members so von

Menges said: 'We don't hold meetings. If something comes up, we put our head round the door and talk about it.'

Other *Vorstand* leaders emerge suddenly in a blaze of publicity only to find they cannot live up to their reputation. Such was the case with Dr Kurt Lotz, successor to the legendary Professor Heinrich Nordhoff at Volkswagen who had built up the company from nothing after the Second World War. Dr Lotz arrived from Brown, Boveri at an unfortunate time and ran into every conceivable difficulty. There was no successor to the Beetle, for years the secret of VW's success, and the company was too dependent on the American market which took about one out of every three Volkswagens produced. There were quarrels within the *AR* and the *Vorstand*. There were plans for new models which never went into production and at press conferences Dr Lotz (by now known as 'Lotz of trouble') would speak only vaguely of investing in the new future (*die neue Zukunft*). At times it seemed that every business magazine in the country was running stories predicting his downfall, most of them based on mysterious leaks from the *AR*. In the end he resigned, to be succeeded by Herr Rudolf Leiding, a man who had come up from the shop floor. Herr Leiding began as a fitter at Wolfsburg just after the war. In the course of his career he had been in almost every part of the organisation including rationalising the VW subsidiary in Brazil which became more profitable than the parent company. Latterly he had been head of the VW subsidiary in Germany, Audi NSU Auto Union, whose Audi models had been giving VW a boost just when it was most needed. Subsequent departures from the *Vorstand* after Dr Lotz had left indicated that the quarrels continued, but that Herr Leiding was tough enough to weather them.

Ruling Shareholders

But who are they, these *AR* members who can make life sweet for a Sohl or a von Menges and so unpleasant for a Lotz? They represent the shareholders and the shareholders in Germany are very mixed in character. They fall into four main groups: the traditional 'small man' who is very often a widow or a pensioner, the banks, the state and the rich families, such as the Haniels, the Flicks, the Quandts or the Thyssens. A big company can be owned by members of any one of these groups or by any conceivable combination of them. The type of ownership does not on the whole seem to be reflected in the company's performance and it is doubtful if anyone could detect it from reading a balance sheet. For example, the big German chemical companies, which have always been highly successful, have been consistently owned by the small man. When I. G. Farben was split up by the Allies, it was said in the Nuremberg judgment that there were 500,000 shareholders. No source was given for the figure which may have been too high, but even if it is taken as 300,000 it gives an average holding of 4,500 *Reichmark* or 0.0003 per cent of the capital stock. The largest known holding in family hands was less than one per cent and there was no industrial holding of more than 2 per cent. The Allies set up three main successors — Hoechst, Bayer and BASF,* plus a few smaller ones such as Casella and Huels. In 1972 Bayer published an analysis of its shareholders which suggests that they totalled 458,000, and that each held an average of 80 shares or 0.0002 per cent of the capital. It was estimated that about 22 per cent of the shares were held abroad, but that there was absolutely no dominant owner. Much the same picture is thought to apply to Hoechst and BASF, and in each case the number has been swelled by the issue of shares to employees. In the engineering sector, a very similar analysis of the company's ownership was given by the chairman of Mannesmann, Dr Egon Overbeck, at the 1973 annual general meeting.

Some of the most detailed work on the spread of ownership, has been done by the Bundesbank.[2] At the end of 1972 there were apparently 5.4 million security deposits (not all of them shares) held by domestic individuals in the banking system. This works out at about one for every four households, though some households of courses will hold more than one account. The total market value of the deposits was put at Dm 90,000 million. According to the Bundesbank, 56 per cent of them had a market value of less than Dm 5,000. About 32 per cent had a value of between Dm 5,000 and Dm 25,000, about 10 per cent a value of between Dm 25,000 and Dm 100,000 and three per cent a value of over Dm 100,000.

Putting the figures the other way round gives a rather different picture, for it becomes clear that the deposits with a market value of less than Dm 5,000 account for only 6 per cent of the total, but that deposits of over Dm 100,000 account for 44 per cent of the total. The Bundesbank concluded that 'security ownership is relatively widely distributed, but that the small holders play a relatively small rôle'. But a

*These three have each become so big that there is no longer any talk of them merging.

study of the statistics did reveal that among the small deposits shares were much more prominent than fixed interest securities – a tribute to the success of the issue of 'People's shares' by the government and of company issues to employees, and also that private individuals were the most important single group of shareholders. At the end of 1972 they held share deposits to a nominal value of Dm 11,500 million or 18.4 per cent of all shares outstanding. The domestic banks, who are often regarded as running the whole show and whom we shall come to later, owned shares of Dm 4,945 million nominal or 7.9 per cent of the total.

The Bayer breakdown shows, and the Bundesbank research bears out its conclusions, that the small shareholder exists in rather surprising numbers, but that he rarely exerts much influence. This situation was brought about by that very German phenomenon – the 'People's share', but it seems unlikely that this phenomenon will be repeated. It came about partly by accident and partly by design because the Federal Government had become a considerable owner of industry. In the late 1950s this seemd incompatible with the climate of the free market economy and the economic miracle (*Wirtschaftswunder*), so the Government, anxious to promote economic democracy, decided to sell. Preussag, the minerals concern which has since fallen on hard times. was chosen first, then part of Volkswagen (an inheritance from the *Reich*) and the energy concern VEBA. The issues were on the whole a great success; the shares were sold at favourable prices and purchases restricted to Dm 500 nominal for any one individual. In the case of Volkswagen the issue was heavily oversubscribed. In theory, the Government could have gone on and sold other properties, but there are some, such as the Salzgitter steel and engineering complex close to the East German border, for whom it would be difficult to find a buyer, and the government did not want to get out of industry entirely. It still holds 40 per cent of VEBA along with about 1.3 million other shareholders. It also still holds 16 per cent of Volkswagen while a further 20 per cent belongs to the Government of Lower Saxony, the state where VW has most of its German plant. Ironically, by 1973 the Government was in the market again, but this time as a buyer. It acquired just over 50 per cent in the oil and chemicals concern Gelsenberg in an attempt to make West Germany more of a force in the international oil world. In these cases representatives of the of the other shareholders – the bankers and so on. In VEBA the Government's voice is said to be decisive, of the other shareholders – the bankers and so on. In VEBA the Government's voice is said to be decisive, despite its holding being less than 50 per cent.

The Power of the Banks

The rôle of the banks in German industry is often exaggerated; it is nevertheless crucial. Public discussion tends to concentrate on the activities of the 'Big Three' — the Deutsche, the Dresdner and the Commerzbank, who between them are responsible for perhaps 15 per cent of all West German credits and deposits. (About 60 per cent are accounted for by institutes owned directly or indirectly by the state.) Like nearly all German banks they are 'all-purpose', indulging in share dealing both on their own behalf and on behalf of their customers, as well as in business which elsewhere would belong to the merchant banks. As the Bundesbank showed, the shareholdings of all the domestic banks was a little less than 8 per cent at the end of 1972. This is probably less than most people believe, but it includes some spectacular properties. The Deutsche Bank owns more than 25 per cent of Daimler-Benz, which it effectively controls with the help of the Flick family. The Deutsche and the Commerzbank each hold more than 25 per cent of Karstadt, one of the country's leading department store chains, while the Commerzbank and the Dresdner each have over 25 cent of another department store chain, Kaufhof. The Big Three are also strongly involved in the construction industry and the Dresdner Bank owns over 25 per cent of the metals concern, Metallgesellschaft. Outside the Big Three a Bavarian bank known as the Bayern-Hypo achieved a certain notoriety in the early 1970s by a series of brewery take-overs to the point where it became known as 'the brewery bank'. (Beer is big business in Germany and the breweries often own large quantities of urban land.) The spokesman for the board, Dr Anton Ernstberger, explained that his bank was trying to break out of Bavaria and in its acquistions policy was simply trying to catch up with the sort of holdings other banks had acquired in the past. His action was not wildly admired in banking circles who were aware that it would increase public criticism of banking activities, and indeed in 1973 the call for the banks to be nationalised became a prominent cry among sections of Herr Brandt's Social Democrat Party.

Herr Franz Heinrich Ulrich of the Deutsche Bank tried to set the record straight, and perhaps to signal a change in policy. It was not the intention of the Deutsche Bank. he told the annual general meeting in 1973, 'to acquire larger holdings of shares to serve interests of our own in industry, to obtain control of industrial and other firms — except financing institutions — or to influence the management. That is why we do not hold the majority in any company or hold a percentage of shares in any company for the purposes of management control.' Herr Ulrich went on to say that the bank not only bought participations but sold them, and was increasingly doing the latter. 'In the years since 1952 the Deutsche Bank has re-sold around four-fifths of the industrial participations it has acquired. We intend to reduce our present holdings further. This aim is consistent with the process of the re-orientation of our business and participation interests towards our international work. Thus in 1972 we sold a further three participations. In 1973 we have so far sold two and not acquired any additional ones.'

In this speech and elsewhere, Herr Ulrich also went into what he regarded as the legitimate relationship between the banks and industry. He made two main points. First, that it was right and necessary for the banks to invest part of their funds in shares 'just as any private individual, any entrepreneur and any other public limited company invests in shares.' Secondly, that the banks had the possibility 'and I think the duty' to help keep the economy in order (*eine Ordungsfunktion*).

'When participations are for sale,' he said, 'where a company might be subject to unwelcome outside influence, where production programmes are to be expanded, in cases of financial reorganisation, new groupings, the formation or the splitting up of partnerships estate settlement and so on, it is often necessary to find a financially strong buyer or partner who can assist in finding a constructive solution. This is the proper role for the banks and it offers them an interesting business opportunity as well.'

When asked in a rather hostile television interview why he did not extend the divestment policy to getting out of Daimler-Benz, Herr Ulrich hedged somewhat and said that the shares had been acquired to prevent foreign participation at a time when they had a much lower market value than today. If the bank sold them it would mean unnecessary profits and unnecessary tax payments. (Under the German tax law the latter point is true.) He maintained that in any case the shares were a good investment. This seems to be the general policy shared by the other big banks: plum industrial holdings will be kept.

Herr Ulrich's summary of the rôle of the banks is right, for at the times when they have intervened in management it has been in their capacity as suppliers of credit* rather than shareholders. This was never

---

*In their function on credit supplies, they have been arguably too liberal and have thus contributed to inflation, or so the Bundesbank would contend.

more strikingly illustrated than in the case of Krupp. In the mid-1960s Krupp was perhaps the best known firm in Germany; it was also an anachronism. It remained a sole proprietorship, the property of Alfried Krupp, who was under no obligation to publish a balance sheet or to reveal the size of his empire. He was believed to be one of the five richest men in the world in company with King ibn-Saud of Saudi Arabia, the Sheikh of Qatar, the ruler of Hyderabad and J. Paul Getty. But there were clouds on the horizon. For one thing his son, Arndt Krupp von Bohlen und Halbach, photographed jet-setting in the world's glossy magazines, showed little sign of following in the family tradition and taking over the firm. For another there was the German mini-recession of 1966–7. There may also have been some resentment among the banking establishment, when it finally moved, at Alfried's plenipotentiary.

To what extent Alfried ran Krupp was never entirely clear. In 1953 he took on an *alter ego* in Herr Berthold Beitz who has played a key role in the company ever since. Beitz is a thoroughly unconventional man by the standards of German industry. He was born in 1913 in Pommerania, trained as a banker, then in 1939 joined Deutsche Shell in Hamburg. For most of the war he ran the Boryslav oil fields in occupied Poland. Afterwards the British gave him a job in insurance. In 1949 he became chairman of the Iduna-Germania, an insurance company which quickly set off on a rapid growth rate. In 1952 he met Alfried for the first time. The almost immediate offer of the job as plenipotentiary came apparently as a complete surprise. Beitz sent for the entire Springer press files on the Krupp concern and on the Ruhr, of which he knew little, before accepting. For the rest of the Ruhr his appointment was a considerable shock. He broke all the rules, publicly revealing he was paid a million Deutschemark a year and showing a way-out taste for jazz and barbecues. He was dubbed 'Der Amerikaner' and called 'Ruhrfremd' (alien to the Ruhr). There was no doubt, however, that he had the most extraordinary *rapport* with Alfried and the two got into difficulties together.

The trouble with Krupp was that it was a throwback to the past. The firm had become great in the early days of the German Industrial Revolution which was based on coal and steel. In the post-war period the coal industry was a sector to be avoided – as Friedrich Flick realised and Alfried Krupp did not. As a sole proprietorship Krupps lacked the access to capital needed both to modernise the old industries like steel and to invest in the new technologies. It was also the prime example of paternalism in its attitude to its workers. The company's

1848876

problems began with the threat of recession. Beitz and Alfried sought
to maintain employment by winning a series of large export orders in
Eastern Europe. There was no difficulty in getting the orders because
Krupp had long been a prestigious name in the East and Beitz, with his
wartime experience, soon acquired an enormous and lasting reputation
there. There was, however, a problem about credit.

Rumours that all was not well began to circulate early. They were
initially played down in the press, but it was the country's best-known
banker, Dr Hermann J. Abs, then the head of the Deutsche Bank, who
first took action. Dr Abs demanded to see a financial statement. The
figures, especially on liquidity, were quite obviously awful. What
followed was a concerted rescue operation mounted by the banks and
the Government, but on strict conditions. The sole proprietorship was
to end. Krupp was to be converted into a joint stock company with all
its shares owned by a Krupp foundation (*Stiftung*). There was to be an
AR and a *Vorstand* just like everywhere else and the banks placed limits
on the amount of export credit. As it turned out, Aflried and Beitz had
been working on the *Stiftung* solution all along, largely because of
Arndt's lack of interest in taking over. During the crisis Arndt
renounced his inheritance, though he was to be entitled to an income of
Dm 2 million a year out of Krupp's industrial earnings for life as a
reward, and Alfried died. From 1968 the house of Krupp was no longer
run by a Krupp, and the bankers had made their most telling
intervention in industry.

But, of course, there are other ways in which the banks can exert an
influence such as through their representation on the *AR*s. In 1966
there was a new law passed known as the *Lex* Abs, after Dr Abs who
belonged to more supervisory boards than anyone else, limiting the
number of *AR*s to which any one individual could belong to ten. In
fact, few bankers nowadays would like to sit on more since membership
does take up valuable time and one wonders if the men from Frankfurt
really enjoy their obligatory journeys to the Ruhr to sit through annual
general meetings.

An analysis of the *AR*s of the country's top nine companies
measured by sales in 1972 shows that out of a total of 168 seats 37
were held by bankers, 23 of whom came from the Big Three. This is
perhaps less than is generally assumed, though the dominance of the Big
Three is clear. Still, as Herr Ulrich points out, the bankers do not elect
themselves; they are chosen by the shareholders. Their position is
bound to give them an influence over company strategy and,
remembering the *AR*'s powers of hire and fire, over the composition of

the *Vorstand*. As the people who know most about the availability of credit, they must have a considerable influence on investment policy. The shareholders seem to like them, and none more than that fourth category to whom we now turn – the rich families.

Flicks, Quandts and Family Power

The most powerful of them all is undoubtedly Flick, though it would be hard for an outsider to tell from reading company reports or even the newspapers. Friedrich Flick KG, founded in 1934, is a holding company in Dusseldorf whose function is to look after – in a very decentralised way – the Flick industrial enterprises. In recent years it has published an annual consolidated balance sheet which reveals little except the group's obvious financial soundness. In 1972 it showed current assets of Dm 2,532 million against liabilities of Dm 2,718 million, most of which are long term and some of which do not mature until the 1990s. Even this was an understatement, for the assets exclude Daimler-Benz on the grounds that the Flick holding is less than 50 per cent. And the brief annual report omits altogether any account of the Flick story.

Friedrich Flick died in 1972 at the age of 89. The son of a Westphalian farmer, he had the distinction of creating a major industrial empire not once but three times. Yet until the Nuremberg Trials his photograph was said never to have appeared in the world press and he remained a relatively unknown figure until the end of his life. He was without social or political ambition and gave as his motivation the simple statement: 'I enjoy working.' Described as 'the genius of silent planning', his talent lay at least as much in selling as in buying, especially when he was in difficulties. His first big success came when be became *Generaldirektor* of the Charlottenhuette in Siegerland, Lower Saxony, in 1915. In the same year he acquired his first shares. He had some money through his wife which enabled him to take over the Charlottenhuette, but the bulk of it came from borrowing at a time of high inflation in order to buy more shares cheaply. Thus in the early 1920s he set about buying up the coal and steel plants in Upper Silesia. At the founding of the Vereinigte Stahlwerke in 1926 he held 36 per cent of Gelsenberg, which was the majority shareholder in the *Verein*. Flick then increased his Gelsenberg holding until he dominated the new steel grouping. In 1931 came the 'Gelsenberg scandal' when the market value of the shares had dropped to 22 per cent of par and it seemed that Flick was in difficulties yet he succeeded in selling them to the state at 90 per cent of par.

If that was the end of the first Flick empire, it was also the beginning of the second. Flick used the proceeds of the sale to buy the Maxhuette, a steelworks outside the *Verein* in Bavaria, and the Harpener colleries in the Ruhr. He was still known from some of his earlier acquisitions as the 'King of Silesia'. This empire was lost under the policy of dismantlement followed by the Allies after the last War. The building of the third empire began only after 1950 when Flick was released from prison by the Allies at the age of 67.

The Allied proceedings against him had been unsatisfactory. Only the Americans participated and a number of charges against him were found not proven, probably because his own simple statement 'I enjoy working' was true. In the 1932 presidential election he had given financial support to Hindenberg, not Hitler. Subsequently he became a member of the Himmler circle of German businessmen and paid 100,000 Reichsmark a year. He said at his trial that he regarded this as a form of insurance. Again he was probably right, for there was no evidence that he had any interest in politics and indeed, like many German businessmen past and present, he seems to have regarded politicians as people who get in the way, but who have to be accommodated. What interested him, however, was the Allies directive to get out of coal. He gladly complied and sold the Harpener collieries to the French concern Sidéchar and another coal holding to Mannesmann. Since the bulk of his possessions had been lost in the east, it was a way of finding capital for new and more moderninvestments. From the sales he emerged at the end of 1953 with nearly Dm 200 million cash in hand.

At the Daimler-Benz annual general meeting in 1955 there was a surprise announcement by Herr Konrad Kaletsch, Flick's cousin and long-time lieutenant; that Flick had acquired over 25 per cent of the shares. About the same time he had been buying the Buderus iron foundries, including Krauss Maffei which was then mainly a locomotive and diesel engine works but which later on produced one of West Germany's few post-war armament successes in the Leopard tank, as well as establishing a solid base in high speed surface transport. Before the end of the 1950s he had acquired control of Feldmuehle, one of Europe's largest paper producers and of Dynamit Nobel, the explosives company originally founded in Germany by Alfred Nobel of peace prize fame, but now concentrating on chemicals and plastics and regarded as one of the jewels in the third Flick empire. After that the policy of

spectacular acquisitions came to an end. There were those who worked
for him who said that he should have gone on and used his wealth to
break into yet more new technologies, such as electronics. But Flick's
view was that the time had come to consolidate the assets he had
already acquired. Besides he was getting old – he was approaching the
age of eighty – and there were problems about the succession. It
appears that he regarded his eldest son Otto-Ernst as lacking the flair to
take over. Otto-Ernst thought otherwise and went to the courts to have
the Flick empire dissolved. In the preliminary judgements the courts
ruled against him and he was eventually bought off by a cash settlement
from his father. In 1966 Friedrich Flick laid down that the bulk of his
industrial possessions should pass to his younger son Friedrich Karl, and
a smaller but still substantial amount to the sons of Otto-Ernst,
Gert-Rudolf and Friedrich Christian. The two grandsons had already
shown the Flick quality of 'enjoying working'.

By 1973 these three seemed to have settled down to a satisfactory
working relationship. They took no more interest in publicity than
Friedrich had done before them. There were no ostentatious displays of
Flick wealth and all the talk was of consolidation. They stuck to the
principle of maximum autonomy for the enterprises within the group
and the Flick name appeared so seldom that a straw poll taken by this
writer in Bonn indicated that few people outside industry and finance
knew who they were, and still less had even the vaguest idea of what
they owned. But if this was true of the Flicks, it was even more so of
West Germany's second richest family of shareholders – the Quandts.

The Quandt group had 1972 sales of Dm 4,800 million against
Flick's Dm 5,700 million (without Daimler-Benz). But the general
ignorance of this name is perhaps more excusable because there is no
formal Quandt group to speak of. Unlike Flick, there is no holding
company, and therefore no need to publish a consolidated balance
sheet. There is simply a Guenther Quandt House in Bad Homburg from
where the business is run. Guenther was the father and founder. Born
into a textile family in 1881, he built up the third largest industrial
empire in Germany after Krupp and Flick. It covered engineering,
armaments, oil and potash, electricals and small holdings in BMW and
Daimler-Benz. When he died during a trip to Egypt in 1954, he left it
equally to his two sons Harald and Herbert, but on condition that they
pool their interests. Harald was the younger and the more interested in
technology; Herbert was practically blind, but it was he who was largely
responsible for the new Quandt interest in BMW which became known
for a time as 'Herbert's model railway'.

The BMW story is exceptional in that it is one of the very few cases in which the Big Banks acting with the majority shareholders were defeated. The original BMW was founded in 1916 to produce aero engines and then motorcycles. Later it built the Austin 7 under licence, but its main car plant was in East Germany and was lost after the war. The company survived, and with it a formidable engineering reputation. But by the late 1950s it was in liquidity difficulties. It was proposed that it should be merged with Daimler-Benz. The chairman of the BMW *AR* was Dr Hans Feith of the Deutsche Bank; the head of the Deutsche Bank Hermann J. Abs, who was also head of the Daimler-Benz *AR*. Not surprisingly, the BMW board urged acceptance of the merger terms at the annual general meeting of 1959. The result had been written off in the press as a foregone conclusion, for the press, like everyone else, had forgotten the small shareholders.

The meeting, when it came, had to be adjourned after a stormy nine and a half hours in which the small shareholders raised one objection after another to the terms. A day or two later Daimler-Benz allowed the offer to lapse.In February 1960 the shareholders elected Dr Johannes Semler, chairman of the Shareholders' Protection Society, to be the new head of the *AR*, the Quandts, who held about 10 per cent, voting in his favour. By the late summer the shares had begun to rocket – not without reason, since in the subsequent reorganisation plan it emerged that the Quandts would play an active role in the future of the company. Some old convertible bonds held by the Quandts were turned into shares and they thus became the key shareholder.

The BMW success story began from there. In 1960 the company had sales worth Dm 239 million. By 1963 when it paid its first post-war dividend they had risen to Dm 440 million and the average yearly sales growth between 1963 and 1972 was 23 per cent. There were no revolutionary changes made. The chaotic organisation, was simply tidied up with the result that success was under way even before new models reached the market. The man who was primarily associated with this success for a decade was Herr Paul Hahnemann, who joined the *Vorstand* in 1961 and developed the 'niche' philosophy – the 'niche' being the market gap between the cars produced by Opel, the German subsidiary of General Motors, and the Mercedes from Daimler-Benz. It was a market based more on psychology than price. 'There are still people,' he said, 'who are willing to pay for the pleasure of driving good cars fast.' Yet even here BMW could produce surprises. In 1969 Herbert Quandt brought in a young man from his own central staff, Herr Eberhard von Kuenheim, to head the *Vorstand*. 'Quandt,' he said on taking over, 'needed someone here whom he knew and who could co-ordinate the board's activities,' the implication being that they were not co-ordinated at present. 'Fast growth,' he added, 'is always untidy.' Hahnemann, the man who had first used the phrase 'Lotz of trouble' for the head of VW, didn't like it. In October 1971 he appeared before Quandt expecting to vindicate his policies and left the interview having been obliged to tender his resignation. It was the chief shareholder, not the chief marketing man, who would run BMW.

The Quandt family produced surprises of its own. In 1967 Harald was killed in a private plane crash, leaving his 50 per cent share of the empire to his wife Inge, and five daughters. Inge wanted security for her family and was not entirely sure that her brother-in-law Herbert would provide it. He might set off on another speculative trip of buying or selling. This problem was settled within the family. In September 1973 there was a brief announcement from Bad Homburg to the effect that Inge had transferred her shares in BMW and the battery concern Varta to Herbert, who in turn had transferred most of his Daimler-Benz shares to Inge. In other holdings, notably the engineering concern Industrie Werke Karlsruhe (IWK), they were to continue to hold equal interests. The arrangement left Inge with a good 10 per cent of Daimler-Benz and Herbert with well over 60 per cent of BMW and 65 per cent of Varta, which alone had sales in 1972 of around Dm 1,600 million. The bulk of the Quandt empire had been effectively split, but there was little public attention for the public had known little enough about the Quandts in the first place. The public was ignorant not because the Flicks and the Quandts evade the law, but because they appear to run their companies much like anyone else. So long as the companies go on producing, providing employment and keeping out of liquidity difficulties the question of ownership scarcely arises.

Although both Friedrich Flick and Guenther Quandt made some contributions to technology in their own right -- it was Flick, for example, who hit upon the idea of feeding waste steel shavings into blast furnaces -- it is for their buying and selling that they will be most remembered. Some of the Krupps, on the other hand, were primarily technologists and the same goes for a number of other families whose names are eponymous with German industry today. For these families the rule quoted at the beginning of this chapter has often come close to what actually happened: 'the first generation builds up the company, the second maintains its position and the third gets into difficulties.' The last part, however, should perhaps be amended to read: 'the third gets into difficulties *unless it takes precautionary measures in time.*'

The Krupps, though they were more than third generation, are the most conspicuous example of a family failing to take account of this principle. As a result, they lost the business altogether.* The Haniels at GHH are a good example of a family which learned the lesson early. They lost the taste for the business but preserved the fruits by turning the management over to professionals. In 1970 they showed they had learned a further lesson – the necessity of being able to call on outside capital for expansion and modernisation. The Allianz, West Germany's largest insurance company, had a 10 per cent stake in the equity. Its industrial share holdings were not large, but its financial soundness was beyond doubt. Thus it was agreed that the holding in GHH be raised to 25 per cent by means of a capital increase. The Haniel stake went down to 35 per cent, but the two interests were pooled. The access to outside capital had been assured, while the family had preserved a strong influence.

Yet even the Haniel case is surpassed by that of Siemens. In the post-war period Siemens has been the most consistently successful, one of the most profitable and certainly the most ambitious of all large German companies. Quite why it should have fared so much better than its chief German rival AEG-Telefunken is not immediately clear, for after all AEG has considerable technical achievements to its credit, such as the PAL colour TV system and the first German nuclear power station. But Dr Gerd Tacke, a former head of the *Vorstand* and now a member of the *AR*, probably put his finger on it in that one word 'ambition'. 'We could have been a nice, comfortable, second-class company,' he said, 'but the decision to go for growth, to break into the world league was taken from the start.' Dr Tacke was speaking of the early post-war period when Siemens, heavily concentrated in Berlin, was in ruins. It was calculated that the entire firm could have been bought for a market value of only Dm 72 million. Yet it did have some assets: it had been great before, it had a fund of good will with the Western Allies because the Siemens family had opposed the Third Reich, the German population was ready to rally round and help the recovery, and soon there was Marshall Aid. Siemens decentralised outside Berlin. In 1950 it had sales of Dm 700 million and a payroll of 81,000, in 1960 sales were over Dm 4,000 million and the payroll 209,000 and in 1970 the figures were Dm 12,647 million and 301,000.

*Of course, if Arndt Krupp von Boklen und Halbach had shown any interest in taking over, it might have been a different story.

The sales forecast for the end of the 1970s is between Dm 25,000 and Dm 30,000 million. Already by 1972 foreign sales have accounted for about half the total.

The ambition was at its most obvious in the determination to break into new technologies, if necessary through co-operation agreements with American companies with which it was anxious to catch up. It did this in the nuclear field with Westinghouse and in data processing with the Radio Corporation of America till RCA itself went out of the business. Siemens spent its first money on data processing as early as 1953. Twenty years later the investment is still not paying off in terms of profits, but the determination is still there and in the wide-ranging agreements made with Philips and the French CII perhaps the goal is nearer. In the power station field it pooled interests with AEG in 1970 to form the joint subsidiary Kraftwerk Union (KWU), which immediately became dominant in Europe. That too has yet to make a profit, but the venture was always seen as essentially long term.

This ambition has come as much from the Siemens family as anywhere else. The company was founded by Werner von Siemens in 1847. One of his descendants has been chairman of the *AR* ever since, down to Peter von Siemens, Werner's great grandson, who was born in 1911 and took over in 1971. The family share in the capital has declined with every capital increase. In early 1974 it was put at about 13 per cent distributed among perhaps 100 family members. Other shareholders were estimated at 330,000, of whom nearly 20 per cent were outside Germany and 45 per cent were domestic individuals. About 65,000, or 20 per cent of the total, were Siemens employees. As a company, it seems to represent the ideal mix between tradition, as exemplified by the continuing family interest and place on the *AR*, and progress, as shown by the growth and technical achievements as well as the employee share in the ownership which produce a corresponding loyalty to the firm.

Between the Krupps who lost and the Siemens who won is Thyssen, whose post-war story was briefly discussed at the beginning of this chapter. August Thyssen (1842--1926) was in his time the greatest steel king of them all, but the Thyssen family was ridden by internal dissension and political misfortune. Born the son of a small industrialist in the Eifel, August founded his first company, Thyssen & Co, in 1871. He was a technologist with a passion for rationalisation or for what nowadays would be known (and indeed were so known at Thyssen after the Second World War) as 'economies of scale', but like Friedrich Flick he also had a nose for credit and his possessions were by no means confined to steel. He became the greatest steel producer in Europe, while showing no interest in issuing shares for that would have meant the payment of dividends — and profits were better re-invested. Having quarrelled with his eldest and favourite son August, who ran off with a Berlin showgirl, he died in 1926 — the year of the founding of the Vereinigte Stahlwerke. He had advised that his empire was to be split up, which it was between his other sons Fritz and Heinrich. Fritz took the steel and Heinrich, having married into the Hungarian nobility, the coal, shipbuilding and banking interests. The latter became known as the Thyssen-Bornemisza group. There has never been any attempt on either side to reunite them.

Fritz Thyssen felt strongly and openly about politics, especially about the terms of the Peace of Versailles. He first met Hitler in 1923 and it was he who introduced him to the Dusseldorf Industrie Club, then as now the rather sombre place where the Ruhr industrialists would gather to discuss their affairs and sometimes hold their press conferences. Fritz became a prominent member of the party long before Alfried Krupp. He recanted too late. In 1938, on the eve of the announcement of the war with Poland, he refused his invitation to attend the *Reichstag*. 'This war,' he cabled back, 'means the end of Germany.' He fled first to Switzerland then to France where he was eventually arrested by the German forces along with his wife Amélie, who was to take over the Thyssen story.

Fritz was deprived of his nationality and his property, and he and his wife spent the war in various concentration camps. The property was restored to him by the Allies, but only under the condition that he deconcentrated it. When Fritz died in Argentina in 1951, he left half to Amélie and half to their daughter Anita, Graefin de Zichy for whom Argentina was home. The gathering up of the lost children began from there, for the chosen instrument, Hans Guenther Sohl, acting in a managerial capacity, had the same ambition to build up a large steel concern as had August Thyssen, who was also the owner, before him. The old empire was put together again and extended. Sohl continued his takeovers after the old steel possessions hadbeen reunited. In 1969 an agreement was made with Mannesmann, that it was to restrict its steel-making activities to pre-materials for tubes, the rest of the materials passing to Thyssen, which in turn passed its tube facilities to Mannesmann. The new tubes company, Mannesmannroehrenwerke, was to be two-thirds owned by Mannesmann and one-third by Thyssen. The arrangement added to Thyssen's steel-making capacity, but it also made Mannesmann one of the largest tube producers in the world although, under the direction of Dr Egon Overbeck, it was pursuing a policy of diversification into the construction of complete plants and plastics. Sohl, on the other hand, has gone always for economies of scale, seeking to supply the customers with every possible kind of steel. Perhaps there was something he could learn from Overbeck, the former general staff officer who after the war had paid his way through Frankfurt university by student jobs, had gone as a virtually unpaid assistant to Metallgesellschaft and whose appointment at Mannesmann in 1962 came as a complete surprise. Sohl anyway changed direction. In 1973, just before Sohl's retirement, Thyssen began the processing through of the takeover of Rheinstahl, one of the largest and oldest engineering concerns in the Ruhr but whose results had been consistently unsatisfactory. In the same year Mannesmann took over Demag, another Ruhr engineering concern whose results had been consistently good, but which suffered from a shortage of capital for expansion. It will be an interesting test of the Thyssen and Mannesmann philosophies to see which of the mergers is the more successful.

Ownership in Trust

The ownership of Thyssen had meanwhile changed as the company re-expanded. Amélie and her daughter put their shares into administering trusts, and in 1960 they also set up the Fritz Thyssen Stiftung to which they gave shares worth (nominal) Dm 100 million and which was to use its dividend revenues for the promotion of natural sciences. Its function as a shareholder, however, was to carry on the concern as Fritz would have wished, and he had in fact proposed such a foundation — at the price of renouncing his entire holding — after the war as a way of keeping the firm together. Amélie died in 1965 at the age of 87, her part of the ownership passing to her daughter. The best breakdown that could be obtained in 1973 was that the Thyssen family administering trust owns a little over 25 per cent, the *Stiftung* about 11 per cent and perhaps 130,000 other shareholders owning the rest. There is little doubt, however, that the company has been run increasingly by Sohl and his chief lieutenant and eventual successor Dr Spethmann, and it was Spethmann who was largely responsible for the Thyssen participation in the Fos coastal steel works in the South of France — a move away from the Ruhr.

The *Stiftung* idea, more American than German, was tried, most successfully and completely by Robert Bosch, the genius of the automobile accessory industry who gave his name to what is today the third of West Germany's electrical concerns. When he died in 1942 he left a detailed will giving the executors 30 years to find a suitable company structure which would keep it going in the spirit of the founder. The solution they arrived at in the 1960s was a *Stiftung* which would own around 85 per cent of the share capital, the rest belonging to the surviving members of the Bosch family. Not the least advantage was that Bosch was able to plough back a large amount of the profits for further investment, and today Bosch is a successful company run by non-family managers.

The idea was also resorted to, as we have seen, at Krupp, but with ironic results. The intervention of banks and government in Krupp affairs in 1967 led to the formation of a *Vorstand* headed by Herr Guenther Vogelsang, formerly of Mannesmann, who was to put things in order, and an *AR* headed by none other than Hermann J. Abs, who was to supervise; and the *Stiftung*, which held all the shares, headed by Berthold Beitz. The most famous book on Krupp,[3] concluded at the close of the 1960s, contains a conversation between Beitz and the author. Beitz prophecies that he will still take over, but Beitz, says the author, was wrong again. In fact Beitz was right. In 1970 Abs retired as chairman of the *AR* and was succeeded by Beitz. He had become not only custodian of the Krupp shares, but also the man with powers of hire and fire. He still had to contend with Vogelsang, who was beavering away at rationalisation and who had a high reputation in the Ruhr. But in 1972 it was announced that Vogelsang would not renew his contract. The two men, who could have complemented each other so well, had finally proved incompatible. Beitz's appointed as head of the *Vorstand* Herr Juergen Krackow who had been notably successful at the Krupp shipbuilding subsidiary A. G. Weser, but he lasted only sixty-eight days before he too ran up against superior powers. For the succession Beitz turned to Herr Ernst Wolf Mommsen, an old Ruhr hand who had lately been state secretary at the Defence and the Finance Ministry under Herr Helmut Schmidt. He is considered an elder statesman and too old and experienced a man to have any ambition of replacing Beitz. Krupp meanwhile remained undercapitalised, making profits in times of boom and losses in times of recession, to which it was all too susceptible. But Beitz himself had become Krupp in all but name, which was perhaps what Alfried wanted.

The fact was that Krupp, like Rheinstahl, has become one of the lame ducks of German industry. There is no criticism of the products and it continues to win export orders, not least in Eastern Europe, but it is structurally weak and the future remains uncertain. Yet in the mid-1970s there is no more thought of closing it down or hiving off the more profitable enterprises than there was in the mid-1960s. It continues to fulfill the main element of the social contract, which has become the modern form of paternalism: it looks after its workers, providing them with a high standard of living and security of employment. If it is low on capital and profits, there are other companies with much sounder financial backers whose results are often no better. The Quandts, for example, had held the Industrie Werke Karlsruhe for decades without any obvious return. The Flicks have seen their paper producer. Feldmuehle, fail to make profits. And even before the energy crisis in the autumn of 1973 investment analysts had concluded that automobiles were no longer a growth industry, yet the Flicks held on to Daimler-Benz and Herbert Quandt entrenched himself in BMW. Even where capital was available there was no capital flight into new industries, though there was a rise in investment abroad where labour was cheaper.

There were those who felt in the early 1970s that West German industry, having gone through more than twenty years of almost continuous expansion, was running out of steam and that the social contract was breaking down. Certainly it faces new problems with the onset of creeping inflation, especially on the wages front. The general economic situation, however, continues to be better than elsewhere in Europe and over three generations German industry has shown a remarkable capacity for survival and to adapt to changing conditions. In the opinion of this writer it is well placed for the fourth generation -- more managers than owners -- to do just as well, at least in comparison with its European neighbours. The reason is that the social contract -- expressed through the extraordinary pattern of all-purpose banks, large and small shareholders, government intervention and the codification of labour and company practices -- remains in force.

CHAPTER 4 ITALY: THE DOMINANCE OF STATE CORPORATIONS

John Earle

'In Italia il processo di concentrazione del capitale e quanto mai avanzato; e in questo processo la mano pubblica ha via via acquistato posizioni decisive.' (From the address by Enrico Berlinguer, the Secretary of the Communist Party to the XIIIth Congress at Milan 13 March 1972.)

More of the Italian economy is under public ownership than in any other western country. An approximate estimate of 55 per cent is sometimes given for the degree of state control over industry, but it is difficult to verify. It is significant, however, that the Communist Party programme avoids any sweeping nationalisation proposals (except for some specific sectors like pharmaceuticals) on the grounds that the state already has sufficient economic power in its hands. The public sector controls not only nationalised services like railways and electricity but three-fifths of steel output, a key share of the oil industry, nearly all shipbuilding, the biggest group of shipping lines, three out of the four largest banks, the national airline, the second automobile manufacturer and the second chemical concern, much of the engineering, nuclear equipment, electronics and aero-space industries, a large slice of the motorways, the telephone network, and so on.

The Government's intention is to use the parastatal corporations as a spearhead both for developing the backward Mezzogiorno (or south) and for promoting technologically-advanced industries, as well as a defence against the threat of foreign takeovers in sensitive sectors. For example the vast Istituto per la Ricostruzione Industriale (IRI) is responsible in the Mezzogiorno for the large Taranto steelworks and a projected new steel complex in Calabria, as well as for Alfa Romeo's Alfa Sud motorcar plant near Naples and a planned aircraft factory, jointly with Fiat, near Foggia. Strategic sectors in which IRI is expanding its interests are electronics and aero-space, food, building, and environmental conservation. One of its least successful subsidiaries is the RAI-TV television broadcasting corporation. For years IRI has been unhappy with its mandate, as it has little practical control over the corporation which is under the political influence of Professor

Amintore Fanfani's faction of the Christian Democrats.

The parastatal corporations performed a valuable rôle during the recession in the early 1970s in going ahead with capital investment projects, particularly in the Mezzogiorno. Italy is still a half-industrialised country, and for years will have to aim for substantial industrial expansion if its economy is to realise its full potential. This is not an easy target when much of private industry, overburdened with losses and debts, is in no fit state to do anything beyond trying to keep afloat.

Of course the parastatal corporations do not have the same anxieties over profit and loss accounts, knowing that the state will always support them. The state supplies them wth capital or 'endowment funds', which Parliament periodically votes to increase. But these funds often represent only a fraction of the corporations capital needs. Most public sector companies go to the capital market for the greater part of their requirements, and their bonds are listed on bourses. They are meant to conduct their operations according to the standards of a private concern, and many have private shareholders alongside the state. They take their management from the business world, not the civil service.

The result is a hybrid of public and private enterprise which, under Italian conditions, has in some cases been extremely successful and which private industrialists on the whole accept. Other parastatal companies however have been less dynamic, showing such typical faults of state-owned bodies as lack of initiative, management ineratia, and subservienceto political pressures.

IRI, the Octopus

The oldest corporation, IRI, owes its origin to fascism and the world depression. It was formed in 1933 to save from bankruptcy three banks – Banca Commerciale Italiana, Credito Italiano and Banco di Roma. Their considerable industrial holdings passed to the new IRI and laid the foundations of its present empire; it still has the same three banks, together with the Roman Banco di Santo Spirito and the Mediobanca merchant bank.

Thanks to the national genius for adaptation, IRI survived the Second World War and prospered. Its main holdings, besides the banks, are in steel (Finsider, with Italsider, Dalmine, Terni, etc.), engineering (Finmeccanica, with Alfa Romeo, Ansaldo San Giorgio, Ansaldo

Meccanico Nucleare, Italtrafo, Aeritalia, etc., as well as Grandi Motori Trieste), electronics and telecommunications (Stet, with Società Italiana Siemens, Sip, Telespazio, Selenia, as well as Italsiel), shipbuilding (Fincantieri, with Italcantieri), shipping (Finmare, with Italia, Lloyd Triestino, Adriatica and Tirrenia), food (SME, with Cirio, Motta, Alemagna, Star), airlines (Alitalia), motorways and construction (Autostrade, Italstat), and TV-broadcasting (RAI).

IRI's chairman since 1960 has been Giuseppe Petrilli, a professor of statistics born in Naples in March 1913. Certain characteristics, such as a pasty complexion and domed bald head, his choice of 'The electric effects of rain upon wet ground' as the subject of his doctoral thesis, and hobbies of listening to classical music and solving problems of higher mathematics, might give an impression of academic remoteness. In fact he has a long record of public service, which began when he became president of one of the largest health insurance institutes at the age of thirty-seven, and was followed by two years, from 1958–60, as Commissioner for Social Affairs at the EEC. A co-ordinator rather than centraliser, he is inevitably in the thick of major economic decisions, but somehow appears to avoid direct involvement in the shadier side of party politics. His fervent Roman Catholicism is reflected in a biographical study written in his spare time of the Elizabethan statesman and Roman Catholic saint, Sir Thomas More.

Another interest of Petrilli's is European unity; he is president of the Italian branch of the European Movement. This faith in Europe, however, he manages to keep separate from the management of an industrial empire; for example, Alitalia was allowed a free hand in buying its new generation of aircraft from American and not European manufacturers. IRI's 150-odd companies are, as far as possible, permitted a wide degree of operational independence. An important rôle in planning and policy formulation is played by IRI's general economic adviser, Professor Pasquale Saraceno.

ENI and the Other Parastatals

It would be difficult to imagine a greater contrast in management style between IRI and, in its heyday, ENI. ENI was founded in 1953 by the late Enrico Mattei, one of Italy's most colourful and controversial figures in the 1950s. A wartime commander of Roman Catholic partisans, he was given the peacetime job of winding up the fascist state oil prospecting agency AGIP. Confidential AGIP reports suggested there

might be hydrocarbons in the Po valley, so in defiance of his brief
Mattei secretly – sometimes at night – drilled till he found methane
gas. By exaggerating the extent of his discovery, he stampeded
Parliament into approving a monopoly for exploration in other
promising areas, and then charged high prices for his product to provide
resources for expanding further. In this way AGIP became the kernal of
ENI, which branched out into chemicals, engineering, nuclear fuel,
textiles, hotels and newspapers.

Mattei had unusual vision and singlemindedness. His vision was that
of providing Italy, hitherto poor in raw materials, with an energy base
for its industry to compete effectively with more advanced countries.
Despite his initial success with gas, he never found adequate domestic
reserves of oil, and had to prospect abroad, offering developing
countries more advantageous terms in order to secure concessions. He
also bought, while the Cold War was raging, crude oil from the Soviet
Union. These tactics brought him into collision with the international
oil companies, or 'seven sisters' as he used to call them.

Mattei's methods were often high-handed and autocratic. To achieve
his objectives, he was prepared to subsidize both supporters and
opponents, and funds went to virtually all political parties. In some
ways he wielded greater power than the weak governments he was
meant to serve. It has been said of him that he was one of the personally
most honest figures in post-war Italy who became one of the biggest
forces for corruption. The comparison which Mattei himself was
reported to like was with Sir Francis Drake, who defied his government's orders to singe the King of Spain's beard.

Mattei died in a private plane crash in 1962. Though a storm raged at
the time, it was hardly surprising that rumours circulated of sabotage.
The corporation's finances were in none too healthy a state, and a
period of retrenchment was advisable. After a time Eugenio Cefis, a
former associate of Mattei, became chairman, and returned to a policy
of expansion, though the old antagonism towards the 'seven sisters' had
gone.

In 1971 Cefis left to become chairman of Montedison, and his place
was taken by Raffaele Girotti, a hydraulics engineer born in 1918.
Though a Christian Democrat, Girotti has not the same reputation as
his predecessors for ability in political wire pulling, being more of a
manager, and ENI has lost some of its former bite. It is intended by the
Government, however, to play a pilot rôle in ensuring national oil and
gas supplies.

A corporation which has expanded recently is EFIM (Ente

Partecipazioni e Finanziamenti Industrie Manifatturiere). Founded in 1962, mainly out of the Breda group of engineering companies, EFIM now has interests in eighty-three companies in sectors such as arms production, helicopters (Agusta), paper, glass, cement, tyres (Firestone Brema), motorcycles (Ducati), motorcar accessories, railway rolling stock, electric equipment, ocean fishing, tourist villages, and food. It is emerging as the country's main producer of aluminium.

Its progress is due to Pietro Sette, an energetic Bari lawyer, who was once a lieutenant of Mattei in ENI and negotiated for him what the 'seven sisters' at the time regarded as revolutionary and unacceptable oil contracts with Middle East producers. Besides heading EFIM, Sette has maintained his connection with ENI, being a member of the board and of its executive management committee.

The other main parastatal corporations are EGAM, a conglomerate with interests in mining and minerals, special steels, and textiles; and EAGAM, dealing with thermal spas and mineral waters.

Family Dynasties

The growth of the public sector is the other side of the coin to the eclipse of the family-controlled business. The common solution, when a family faces calls for financing, technological research, or management capabilities that are beyond its resources, is to sell out, either to a foreign concern or, more commonly, to the state. It is not possible, as in some countries, to sell holdings in a business to a commercial bank, as this was specifically prohibited in the banking reform of the thirties, which restricted commercial banks to short-term lending. They manage, however, to get round this to some extent by setting up financial subsidiaries which engage in merchant banking, including taking industrial participations. The Mediobanca merchant bank, for example, is a subsidiary of the three big IRI banks. The public credit institute IMI (Istituto Mobiliare Italiano) has become increasingly involved with well-known companies, such as Olivetti, Zanussi, the SIR chemical group, and Fonditalia, a mutual fund which it took over when the IOS empire failed.

Nevertheless a number of family dynasties are still firmly entrenched. The Agnellis are the biggest private employers in the country, and among the richest families of Europe. Fiat has always been the brightest jewel in their crown. Founded in 1899 as Fabbrica Italiana Automobili Torino, it now has a payroll in Italy of about 190,000.

Besides erecting plant for third parties, like the Soviet Union's largest automobile factory at Togliatti on the Volga, Fiat controls or has joint shareholdings in manufacturing plant in numerous foreign countries. Its interests spread much wider than motorcars; it produces steel, tractors and agricultural machinery, aircraft and space equipment, marine and other engines, nuclear power equipment, turbines, railway locomotives and rolling stock. Fiat owns the leading Turin newspaper, *La Stampa*, and one third of the widest circulating newspaper, *Corriere della Sera* of Milan. Its main manufacturing plant is in the Piedmontese capital of Turin, whose economy to a great extent depends on it, though in recent years the firm has opened new plant in the south.

The Agnellis control Fiat through their family holding company IFI (Istituto Finanziario Industriale), which also has substantial share-holdings in a host of other activities, such as retail stores (Rinascente), insurance (SAI), publishing (Fabbri), ball-bearings (Riv-SKV), vermouth (Cinzano), cement, motorways, banking, the Sestrière wintersports resort and Juventus, Turin's first division football club. Fiat is quoted on stock exchanges, and since 1968 a minority share of IFI has also had a bourse listing.

Fiat's chairman is Giovanni ('Gianni') Agnelli born in 1921 and the managing director is his younger brother Umberto, born in 1934. Their father Edoardo, died young and in the period of post-war recon-struction Fiat was under the autocratic rule of Vittorio Valletta, a pint-sized, self-made man. But, after Valletta's death, Gianni took over the chairmanship in 1966, and the former playboy's views now command attention as those of one of Europe's most influential industrialists. By the standards of most Italian businessmen, the Agnellis are forward looking and enlightened. They are as interested in prob-lems outside as inside Italy, though not all their foreign operations have been a success; for example, attempts to bring Citroën into their net came to naught. Latterly one of their main areas of expansion has been in publishing, newspapers and means of influencing public opinion.

The Agnellis have enough power to be uncomfortable bedfellows to governments and to smaller industrialists, who are often suspicious of their motives. Their relations with labour have deteriorated in recent years. Though Fiat was one of the first firms to experiment with methods to reduce assembly line boredom, it has been a major target for industrial action, partly, perhaps, just because it is the biggest private firm in the country, partly because the Valletta era left a legacy of resentment at impersonal administration, and partly because the unions see Fiat as guilty of attracting thousands of work-hungry immigrants from the south to Turin where no proper housing or social services may await them.

Another northern dynasty now in the third generation are the Pirellis. Leopoldo Pirelli, the chairman, born in August 1925, is grandson of Giovanni Battista Pirelli, who in 1872 set up a factory to manufacture rubber goods in Milan, in the area where the Pirelli skyscraper now stands. The firm started with a capital of 215,000 lire, and Giovanni Battista allowed himself a monthly salary of 250 lire – enough today to buy two bottles of beer. The story goes that the authorities, in their attempts to salvage a sunken naval vessel by pumping air into it, had had to buy rubber tubing from France, and young Pirelli, a 25-year-old patriot who had fought with Garibaldi, was determined that such tubing should be made in Italy. It must have been a hazardous venture, along with many others which failed in those heady years after Italy's political unification, for motorcars were still a thing of the future. But Pirelli was lucky, being ready to profit from this new source of demand through the manufacture of pneumatic tyres, first for bicycles and then, from 1899, for motorcars. His second winning card was expansion into cable and cable laying, particularly under the sea, taking advantage of the spread of telegraphic communications.

The present chairman, Leopoldo, works from an office on the 30th floor of the wafer-thin 34-storey skyscraper near the main railway station. The Milanesi say that the only reason why the skyscraper, which replaced the group's headquarters bombed out during the Second World War, was not built higher was out of respect for the Virgin Mary's statue on top of the gothic cathedral. Leopoldo has the reputation of liking sailing, golf and fast cars, but the family are more withdrawn in their life style than the Agnellis. After taking a degree in mechanical engineering at the Milan polytechnic, Leopoldo went through the works and then ascended the hierarchy, succeeding his father Alberto as chairman in 1965.

Pirelli is as internationally minded as Fiat, with plant in many countries, particularly Europe, the Mediterranean, and Latin America. After all, as far as tyres are concerned, concentration on Italy would have brought an unhealthy dependence on Fiat, which for years has provided two out of three cars on Italian roads. The Pirelli group had 80,500 employees – 41,000 of them in Italy – and eighty-two factories in the world when it negotiated an ambitious cross-frontier merger with Dunlop which came into force in January 1971. The 'union', as the merger was called, was soon strained to nearly breaking point, for

Pirelli's Italian manufacturing company, Industrie Pirelli, immediately accumulated enormous losses.

The union was based on the transformation of the two parent companies, Dunlop and Pirelli, into holding groups which took substantial minority cross-shareholdings in the operational subsidiaries of the other. The union was saved by Dunlop writing off its commitment in Industrie Pirelli, for whose rescue the Italian parent was left solely responsible. It is interesting to speculate whether Pirelli would have survived had the union with Dunlop not been negotiated. Its troubles sprang from the combination of a general recession in the Italian economy, bad labour relations, and management error in putting on the market a radial tyre which, while excellent in road holding qualities, wore out too quickly. Probably the firm would have continued to exist, but under some form of public control, as the Government could hardly have afforded to let such a major firm crash and put its workers out of a job.

At the time, the union was hailed as a courageous attempt at European trail blazing, and a possible pattern for further linkups between European companies. In the event, its vicissitudes seemed to underline the difficulties rather than the advantages of such mergers. The union suffered a further blow in March 1973 when Leopoldo was seriously injured in a motorcar accident in which his elder brother Giovanni died, and he was out of action for seven months. His absence, however, did not prevent plans going ahead for a management shake-up and for the rescue of Industrie Pirelli, while group morale was improved by the disclosure in summer 1973 of a project for a revolutionary new triangular-shaped tyre design needing no inner tube.

The Corporate Entity

The family is no longer in control at Olivetti, Europe's largest manufacturer of typewriters and office equipment, including small electronic calculators and information systems. In some ways the family's leadership has been missed, for it was far in advance of its time in promoting for its employees social insurance, housing, working conditions, and cultural and recreational amenities; though there was a strong element of paternalism, which would not go unchallenged today. The firm has also gained an outstanding reputation for product design and the architecture of its buildings.

The Olivettis were outsiders; Jewish, socialist, and near revolutionaries. Camillo, the founder, was born Samuel David Camillo Olivetti, son of an agricultural merchant from near Ivrea, a pleasant country town at the gateway to the Alpine Valle d'Aosta in the north-west. A fervent socialist, he was detained during riots in Milan in 1898 when aged twenty-nine, and there was a police file on him as a potential subversive. His first business venture was a firm called CGS to make measuring instruments, the initials for centimetre, gram and second. Then in 1908 he set up a limited partnership, Ing. C. Olivetti e C, to manufacture his own design of typewriter. It was at first regarded as a costly curiosity, but sales nevertheless expanded, first to the Government, and then to private clients.

After the First World War, the firm did not escape the labour disorders prevalent throughout industry. But, it is related, they were disorders with a difference, as Camillo Olivetti, already a father figure, freely allowed the workers to occupy the factory if they wished; which they did, but only after insisting that Camillo and the management occupy it with them.

Like many industrialists, Camillo Olivetti saw at first in fascism a return to law and order. But his acceptance of it gradually turned to opposition; and in 1928 his passport was withdrawn. He retired in 1938, handing over the chairmanship to his son Adriano and died, a venerable white-bearded patriarch, in 1943.

Adriano, an unusual combination of businessman and dreamer, headed the firm's expansion after the Second World War both at home and abroad. Under him the first steps were taken to acquire the ailing Underwood Corporation as a basis for expansion on the other side of the Atlantic. Then, in 1960, he died suddenly. The firm went through a crisis following his death. Underwood required a major effort for its rescue, while Olivetti's resources were strained by the need to expand its computer division. To make matters more difficult, the Italian economy was going through a recession. The family relinquished control and accepted help from a group of outside interests, headed by the public finance institute Istituto Mobiliare Italiano and including Fiat, Pirelli and Mediobanca, whose representatives sit in the controlling shareholders' syndicate alongside members of the Olivetti family.

The chairmanship was taken by Bruno Visentini, a lawyer from the Veneto, who is a taxation expert, a former vice-chairman of IRI, and a Republican party member of Parliament. Roberto Olivetti, son of Adriano, is a vice-chairman, and three members of the family sit on the 11-member board. It is a highly internationalised company, with twenty-one factories (eleven in Italy) and a work force of 73,000

(33,000 in Italy). Besides several Latin American countries, the main foreign production centres are in Glasgow, Harrisburg (Pennsylvania), Toronto and Johannesburg. Labour relations in Italy are much better than the average, and the annual general meetings have been described as the most Anglo-Saxon in atmosphere of any held south of the Alps.

Nevertheless, the future is by no means assured. The new management decided that they had not the strength to compete with the giants on the other side of the Atlantic in large computers, and the computer division was sold first to General Electric, and subsequently to Honeywell. The economic downturn of 1969 compelled the company to pass that year's dividend. In 1971 control of the SGS semi-conductor subsidiary was taken over by IRI. Though Olivetti's activities are world wide and its reputation is high, it will have an uphill struggle against American and Japanese competitors. Their resources in the increasingly sophisticated electronic technologies are so much vaster than those of a company whose heart remains in Italy, a semi-developed economy of 54 million people.

Zanussi has followed much the same course as Olivetti, only in a shorter period of time. It embodied all the dynamism of the so-called Italian miracle when it exploded into becoming Europe's — if not the world's — biggest manufacturer of domestic appliances. Pordenone with its 44,000 inhabitants came to depend on it economically as Ivrea does on Olivetti or, on its larger scale, Turin on Fiat.

The founder Antonio Zanussi died in 1946, and was succeeded by his sons Guido and Lino, but Lino was the genius who put Zanussi on the map. In 1954 production was expanded from cookers into refrigerators, in 1958 into washing machines, and in 1960 into television sets and electronics. Co-operation and production agreements were entered into with leading companies abroad such as AEG-Telefunken of West Germany, Hoover in Britain and General Electric of the United States. At home the company developed an enormous appetite, taking over rivals such as Becchi, Stice, Aspera, Castor, Zoppas and Triplex. But before this process was completed, Lino and some of his closest associates were killed in an accident to their private aircraft in Spain in 1968.

This was the first of a series of mishaps. The economy went into a three-year recession in 1969, and the firm was not spared the serious industrial unrest that swept industry. Guido Zanussi did not get on with the new Roman-born chief executive, Lamberto Mazza, a former bank manager, and resigned the chairmanship in favour of Mazza. The company was unable to implement its plans for full scale production of colour TV sets, because the Government procrastinated for years on which colour TV system to adopt. Lino's widow and other members of the family became involved in litigation brought by the authorities over alleged evasion of duty on Lino's estate.

The 1970 results showed a tiny profit, and the 1971 figures a serious loss. A bank consortium headed by the state-controlled Istituto Mobiliare Italiano intervened to lend 50,000 million lire against deposit of 49 per cent of the capital, while AEG-Telefunken advanced funds amid rumours that it planned one day to take the firm over. Zanussi had been brought to its knees, but in 1973, signs appeared that, under a reorganisation plan drawn up by Mazza, it is beginning to rise to its feet again.

Montedison, the chemical giant and second biggest private firm in the country after Fiat, owes its rescue from disaster to Eugenio Cefis, former chairman of ENI, who in consequence has become one of the most powerful personalities in the economy. The company was in a bad way when Cefis accepted the chairmanship in the spring of 1971; he sought the post, apparently as a personal challenge.

He is a strangely shy man: during his chairmanship of ENI the press office was not allowed to distribute his photograph. For years a favourite retreat was a coffee plantation in Tanzania. Collaborators say he likes, when concentrating on a problem or negotiation, to be driven round in a car without any particular destination.

Montedison was born in 1966 from a virtual takeover of the long-established chemical concern Montecatini by the north Italian electrical utility Edison, another old company which was flush with capital from the nationalisation of electricity. The merger was not a success. Montecatini had been too accustomed to protectionism from pre-war fascist attempts at self-sufficiency, and Edison to the monopoly conditions of supplying electricity. The two managements did not get on with each other. Though it was well known that Montedison was financing the political world, some of its top executives' activities were of a particularly questionable nature and later came under judicial investigation. The Press subsequently reported magistrates' investigations linking Giorgio Valerio, the former chairman, with secret 'black funds' and with a mysterious deal over the supply of substandard radio sets to the armed forces.

Cefis applied drastic medicine to Montedison. He found the shareholders up in arms, not so much over the serious situation of the group — the old management used to keep them happy with an annual dividend without revealing much of what was going on — as over the fear that a process of surreptitious share buying, instituted by Cefis himself in his former ENI capacity, would bring back-door nationalisation. Cefis managed to overcome much of their discontent by initiating a regular policy of disclosing information, while bluntly warning that for some years they could expect no dividends. He fought a running battle with his former companion, Raffaele Girotti, to keep ENI at arm's length.

Inside the group Cefis restructured its activities, concentrating on the four priority sectors of chemicals (rationalised under the parent company), fibres (setting up Montefibre), food (forming Alimont) and retailing (retaining the Standa chain stores), while selling off companies of peripheral interest. New management was brought in. Montedison's reserves were fully drawn on and the share capital was halved. Emphasis was given to deals with foreign countries, such as the supply of plant and factories to the Soviet Union, in what had always been a rather inward-looking group. Financial and commodity markets were speculated in with success.

The price of writing off obsolete plant and cutting off the dead wood, in addition to current unprofitable trading, was a staggering loss of over £400 million ($960 million) reported between 1970 and 1972, of which 458,500 million lire (then worth £305 million) fell in 1972. Critics, particularly rivals in the chemical industry, claimed that Cefis overdramatised in order to make his subsequent achievement all the greater, and that common sense plus improved world conditions would have brought the group round anyhow. But Cefis has provided much needed leadership, at times ruthless, as when he closes factories and puts people out of work in order to bring pressure on Rome. He has also his private friendships with Rome politicians, and has emerged as one of the more formidable figures on, or rather behind, the national scene.

The Entrepreneurs

However reticent by nature, Cefis cannot avoid the limelight to the same extent as Attilio Monti, the leading independent oil refiner, sugar baron and newspaper proprietor. Now one of the country's richest men, Monti started life in 1907 as the son of a Ravenna blacksmith.

A travelling salesmanship in mineral oils brought him as a young man into contact with Ettore Muti, then fascist boss of Ravenna and later national secretary of the fascist party. Ever since, Monti has been credited in the Press with views well to the right of centre, but he does not take any public interest in politics. He was a businessman from the start, becoming proprietor of a petrol and oil storage depot in Ravenna's small port. Though the depot was damaged during the war, Monti was there to receive the first post-war tankers. Borrowing money, he expanded into oil refining, a network of petrol service stations, and purchase of control of the Pibigas company distributing bottled gas. The latter provided a useful cash flow, as he insisted on the user making a deposit on receipt of each bottle.

A deal with BP in 1957 gave useful stability, as BP rented the service stations and provided a guaranteed outlet for Monti's refining operations. In 1973 he bought back BP's activities when that company decided to cut its losses and withdraw from Italy. In due course Monti expanded to the south, through the purchase of Paul Getty's local operations and the construction, with help of Cassa per il Mezzogiorno incentives, of what was then the country's biggest refinery at Milazzo in Sicily. Supertankers were bought to bring the crude oil for refining and, looking further afield, a project was submitted in the early 1970s for a combined oil refining and steel complex on the Scottish coast at Hunterston, Ayrshire.

The story goes that Monti went into beet sugar because he wanted to buy a newspaper, *Il Resto del Carlino* of Bologna, and it formed part of the group owning Eridania, the biggest sugar refining company accounting for one third of the Italian output. Besides *Il Resto del Carlino*, Monti's chain consists of *La Nazione* of Florence, *Il Telegrafo* of Leghorn, *Stadio* (a sports daily) of Bologna, and *Il Giornale d'Italia*, a Rome evening paper. Eridania has also ramifications into farming, animal foodstuffs and grain storage.

Widower and vegetarian, Monti is a controversial figure, although he usually manages to sidestep public controversies. Some of his oil refining operations, like those of other companies, have aroused polemics on environmental grounds. Eridania is one of the European sugar companies involved in trouble with the EEC for alleged restrictive practices to restrain competition. Though Italian processors receive special subsidies, the consumer is accustomed to paying higher prices than in other Community countries. No love is lost between Monti and the Communist authorities administering his home region of Emilia-Romagna, especially as he owns the main newspapers in the 'red belt, across central Italy. With his personal jet aircraft, yachts, and residences in Italy and abroad, Monti is an example of what the left sees as a reactionary capitalist, yet he manages to live very well from his activities in Western Europe's largest area ruled by the Communists.

Monti is one of a race of independent operators who sprang up when Italy, lying between the Middle East and Western Europe, became Europe's largest oil refiner. Others include Angelo Moratti, who has expanded to Jamaica and incidentally possesses a third of *Corriere della Sera* of Milan, and Riccardo Garrone of Genoa, while Nino Rovelli has based his refining operations in Sardinia.

Rovelli dislikes being put in the same class as the men engaged in the rat race of buying and selling. He is not a merchant, but uses his own oil. Under him Società Italiana Resine (SIR) and its associate Rumianca have developed into the third largest petro-chemical group behind Montedison and ENI's ANIC.

SIR's history began when, as an early plastics manufacturer in 1931, it bought the old Italian Bakelite Company. Rovelli, an engineer from Milan, took charge in 1948. In the 1950s SIR expanded in chemicals, and bought the Brill shoe polish company. In the 1960s it developed into petro-chemicals, setting up in 1962 the petro-chemical complex of Porto Torres on what had been desolate northern Sardinian pasture-land. Rovelli's policy has been to form an integrated, vertical group, so that his activities now extend from prospecting for oil – unsuccessfully – and conveying it in his tankers from the Persian Gulf, to manufacturing a host of chemical and petro-chemical products, among the latest of which are man-made textiles, synthetic rubber and motor tyres, and prefabricated building components. Lack of water at Porto Torres caused him to design his own desalination plant, while another sideline of his is newspaper ownership in Sardinia.

Born in 1917, Rovelli is a family man with four small children; women see in him a resemblance to Clark Gable. There is something in him of the restless dynamism and aggressiveness of Mattei, though Mattei was basically a shy man while Rovelli is an extrovert who will dominate a conversation. Under him SIR has usually managed to report annual rises in turnover of at least 20 per cent, even in bad years for the economy as a whole. SIR puts on a David and Goliath act in taking on both Montedison and ENI, whom it accuses of making use of their greater political influence. It has on occasion clashed with both at the same time, as when it went ahead with a scheme of its own in 1972–3 for man-made fibres production in central Sardinia, despite the presence of a joint ENI-Montedison venture for the same purpose a few miles away. Rovelli has been helped by close working links with Istituto Mobiliare Italiano and, probably, by his shrewdness in setting up a series of different companies for the Porto Torres complex; each of which, while integrated with the others, was able to make maximum use of the incentives for investing in the Mezzogiorno.

The Financiers

Italy provides ideal terrain for financiers who wish to remain in the shadows. It offers ample opportunities for uninformative company reports, for balance sheet window dressing, and for cross holdings blocking outside takeovers. Some important companies even keep secret the identity of their real owners. Such is the case with Liquigas, the fourth largest chemical concern.

Carlo Pesenti is a financier of the old school. He was born in 1907 near Bergamo, and his empire was founded on the family firm, Italcementi, the largest cement manufacturer in the country. It comprises Italmobiliare, set up in 1946 as a financial holding company, about which Pesenti discloses little; another holding company, Bastogi; a number of provincial banks and also Istituto Bancario Italiano, which he established in 1967, to rescue from failure a group of small banks owned by a Christian Democrat senator, thereby saving the party from possible scandal. The empire extends to important holdings in insurance (Riunione Adriatica di Sicurtà), steel (Falck), engineering (Franco Tosi), to a seat on the Montedison controlling shareholders' syndicate, as well as to the newspapers *La Notte* (a Milanese right wing evening paper) and the local *Il Giornale di Bergamo*.

As people who wish to remain anonymous sometimes end up by attracting more gossip, the Italian press likes to recount stories about him which may or may not be true; of a former amateur boxing champion said to act as his bodyguard; of an electric blanket switched on in bed in all seasons, summer as well as winter; of spiritual retreats at a Trappist monastery above the French Riviera. Bald and pale, Pesenti is reported to have a heart condition.

Pesenti is a centraliser by nature, and is said to allow only limited authority to his son Gianpiero, who is married to the daughter of a Nobel prize winner for chemistry, Giulio Natta. He has always been on close terms with the Bergamo archbishopric and the financiers of the Vatican.

In recent years, his empire was thought widely to be on the decline, particularly after he suffered two notable defeats. In 1968 Michele Sindona, the young Sicilian financier, managed to buy enough

Italcementi shares to threaten Pesenti's dominance, and Pesenti had to buy them from him at a high price. Then in 1969 the Turin motorcar manufacturer Lancia, which he had purchased from the Lancia family, was saved from disaster only by the intervention of Fiat, which bought it for a purely nominal value of one lire a share. But in 1973 Pesenti bounced back by taking effective control of the large financial holding company Bastogi, through buying Montedison's holding, thanks to a new alliance with Montedison's chairman, Eugenio Cefis.

Among the present generation there are at least three operators whose activities or rumoured activities are enough to make shares on the small Milan stock exchange bob wildly up or down – Roberto Calvi of Banco Ambrosiano; Anna Bonomi Bolchini, a shrewd business mind who started with real estate interests in Milan and has broadened into property in Italy and abroad, banking and finance, matches, soap and detergents, and mail order, and Michele Sindona.

Sindona, born in 1920 at Patti near Messina in Sicily, is disliked by many in the financial establishment as an upstart who they regard as sailing close to the wind, but they have failed to prevent him building up a large personal fortune. He has bought and sold more companies than any other Italian living. His philosophy is simple – buy cheaply, and sell at a profit. He is not interested in an industry or in running a company, so much as in making money out of it. Not everything he has touched has turned to gold. Nevertheless, his rivals admit that he has shown, not only courage bordering on recklessness, but an unparalleled 'fiuto' or 'nose'.

After starting as a lawyer in Messina, the 'avvocato' moved to Milan's broader horizons in 1947. His expertise in company taxation brought him to the attention of Snia Viscosa, the man-made fibres company who in due course offered him a seat on the board, and of American businessmen wishing to expand activities in Italy but bewildered by the tax jungle.

There is little point in trying to list the companies he has bought and sold. His present empire in Italy – always subject to what he may buy or sell tomorrow – appears to be based on Banca Privata Finanziaria and Banca Unione of Milan, Banca di Messina of Messina, and a huge property empire grouped under Società Generale Immobiliare, which incidentally numbers the Watergate complex in Washington among its numerous foreign assets. In 1973 he was building up Finambro as a possible umbrella for many Italian activities.

Abroad, Sindona owns Fasco A.G. of Liechtenstein, and its subsidiary Fasco International of Luxembourg, as well as Banque de

Financement of Geneva. In the United States, where he moved his headquarters for a time after the failure of a takeover bid for Bastogi, Sindona has practical control over Franklin New York Corporation, which embraces Franklin Bank of New York; another financial group, Talcott National Corporation; as well as some industrial companies with names like Oxford Electric, Interphoto, and Argus.

Sindona has had close contacts with the Vatican, treading on the toes of Carlo Pesenti by becoming one of their confidential advisers for a time. He bought control of Società Generale Immobiliare from the Holy See, and helped the Church to get rid of some of its less profitable Italian shareholdings, diversifying their interests more abroad. At one time or another he has worked intimately with a number of well-known finance houses and conglomerates, including Hambros Bank, Continental Illinois Bank, Gulf and Western, and Banque de Paris et des Pays-Bas.

Don Michele is married to a girl from his own village of Patti. Other Italians find him cold and calculating, as Sicilians sometimes appear. A non-smoker, he has a habit during conversation of folding paper hats and boats one after the other, which he does by touch, so that he can look his partner in the eye. But, more important than his eyesight, is his feel for a profit.

Vatican Wealth

Much nonsense has been written about the Vatican's wealth and the ways in which it allegedly uses or misuses its financial power. At least part of the blame for this can be laid at the door of the Vatican itself. It is one of the few states in the world that does not present a budget, and its officers from cardinals downwards display an almost furtive passion for secrecy.

The Roman Catholic Church claims 653 million believers throughout the world, whose spiritual needs are ministered to by an army of 1.5 million priests and men and women in religious orders. Without doubt, in its two thousand years of existence it has amassed a vast amount of assets, in the form of real estate, art treasures, inherited wealth and stocks and shares. Most of these material belongings, however, are not administered centrally from Rome, but by local churches and catholic organisations.

The foundation for the Vatican's own financial wealth was laid by the 1929 Lateran Pacts, which set up the Vatican City State, thus composing the dispute which had lasted since 1870 between the Kingdom of Italy and the Papacy. As compensation for property expropriated by the Italian state, the Vatican was given 750 million lire in cash and 1,000 million lire in 5 per cent Italian state bonds, both of which were worth very much more than today. Part of the cash was spent on buying office and residential space required by the new structure of the Holy See, while the rest was invested, nearly all in Italy.

Such was the situation until the late 1960s. The Vatican was fortunate in benefiting from the advice of several successful Italian financiers, such as the late Bernardino Nogara of the Banca Commerciale Italiana who handled its investment activities from 1929 onwards, or more recently Massimo Spada, who sits on the boards of a series of leading banks and insurance companies. It accumulated important and in some cases controlling holdings in a number of Italian companies, especially those based in Rome, such as the Società Generale Immobiliare property giant, the Condotte D'Acqua construction firm, Pantanella (pasta) and Ceramica Pozzi (sanitary fittings). Some, like Immobiliare, did extremely well, while others, like Pantanella and Pozzi, ran into difficult times during the 1960s.

During this period the Vatican found its financial commitments growing – the Vatican Council from 1962–5 alone cost a considerable amount of money – and faced the need to maximise income at a time when the first signs were appearing of accelerating inflation and currency upheavals in the western world. Under Pope Paul VI, therefore, the Vatican finances were reorganised and from about 1968 an active policy was instituted of diversifying shareholdings away from Italy. The services were used temporarily of outside financiers like Michele Sindona, who for example helped to dispose of a sizeable package of shares in Società Generale Immobiliare to Gulf and Western.

The whole operation now resembles that of a large investment trust, run on conservative lines, with holdings in blue chip companies on each side of the Atlantic. As a matter of policy, the Vatican no longer controls companies, but limits itself to minority holdings. In a rare comment on the subject, a senior prelate in 1970 defined investment policy as resting on the three criteria of (1) security of capital, (2) maximisation of income, and (3) avoidance of speculation.[4]

The reorganisation put the Vatican's financial affairs in the hands of three offices. The Prefecture for Economic Affairs, set up in March 1968 under Cardinal Egidio Vagnozzi, a former Apostolic Delegate in Washington, has overall policy control and supervision. The

Administration of the Patrimony of the Holy See, also established in 1968 from a merger of existing offices, is headed by Monsignor Giuseppe Caprio and undertakes the detailed administration that would in a government be performed by a finance ministry. One section deals with investments.

The third body, the Institute for Religious Works (Istituto per le Opere di Religione), is the Vatican's bank. It acts, not only for the Holy See, but also for Vatican residents and employees and for Church bodies and organisations, though it will not open an account for an ordinary member of the public. The funds it handles, therefore, are more extensive than those of the Holy See itself. The secretary is a burly, six-foot American priest born in 1922, Archbishop Paul Marcinkus from Cicero, Illinois.

Much ingenuity has been exercised in trying to discover the size of the Vatican's investments, but they have mostly gone little beyond guesswork. From hints dropped by authoritative prelates, $500 million would appear to be not far from the mark as cost value of investments, at least of those handled by the Administration of the Patrimony of the Holy See, without necessarily comprising those of the Institute for Religious Works. Of these, it would appear plausible to suggest that between $100 and $160 million were retained in investments in Italy. Judging from the movements of most stock market indices in recent times, their performance may not have been exciting in the last few years. On the other hand the Vatican's numerous properties have undoubtedly shared in the big increases in real estate values. At the same time, it should be remembered that many of these do not provide significant income, being occupied rent free or at low rents by offices and people connected with the Church.

CHAPTER 5 GREAT BRITAIN: MONEY MAKERS V THING MAKERS

Anthony Rowley

Financiers flourish only when
nations decline.
. . . Talleyrand.

Britain's industrial structure is the oldest established in Europe and yet, paradoxically, it appears to be the most seriously in need of continuity and stability. Britain was the first country to undergo an industrial revolution, and Europe was able to learn some valuable lessons from the British experience which are still reflected in certain essential differences between the Continental and the British tradition. Whether the legacy of discontent and disenchantment from the Industrial Revolution can be removed by reforms some two centuries after that event in Britain remains to be seen. If not, then something not far short of a second revolution looks likely sooner or later.

Meanwhile there has been no shortage of scapegoats to blame for the industrial and economic ills besetting Britain – inept management and grasping, power-hungry trades unions being the two most frequently cited. Perhaps there is something in these arguments, but to see them as a complete explanation is too simplistic, particularly when they simply emphasise the need for more American-style professionalism on both sides of industry and ignore Britain's part European social tradition. Such arguments also tend to ignore factors like the now apparent deficiencies in the U.K. capital market as it affects industry – deficiencies which are by no means common to the rest of Europe.

The post-war decades have seen an almost unending series of attempts to patch up the threadbare fabric of industry. Trade union reform and the improvement of labour relations has been repeatedly attempted by successive governments without any spectacular success, and American-style business schools have been encouraged to propagate more sophisticated management techniques, again though without any really convincing result. Industrialists have been exhorted to invest more, to export more, to improve their marketing and generally to become more competitive in world markets. Attempts have been made to interest the worker in owning shares in his company and to persuade the big financial institutions that they should use their substantial shareholdings to pressurise inefficient management. In retrospect it is possible to see a confusion of objectives in all this and a failure to grasp certain fundamental shortcomings of the industrial system.

Meanwhile the Stock Exchange, focal point of the City of London, has gone from strength to strength. It has become the theatre of operations for a whole new breed of take-over bidders, asset strippers and share dealers whose real contribution to the economic wealth of the nation is increasingly being called in question. At the same time paternalism as a mode of industrial management has slipped sharply out of fashion without being replaced by any satisfactory and equal professional relationship between the two sides of industry. And family ownership in business has been all the time on the decline under the triple pressures of inflation-fed financing needs, death duties and the liquidity problems of family shareholders. What is sometimes rather flatteringly called a mixed economy in Britain has become something of a ragbag of different and often conflicting interests.

The New Capitalism

An attempt at radical reform, at introducing a new form of pure and abrasive capitalism was made by the Conservative Government on taking office in 1970. It was supposed to be a kind of cultural revolution to rid the land of Socialist revisionism and pluralistic economic doctrines. There was to be no help from the state any more for industrial 'lame ducks'. The new era of laissez-faire proved to be short-lived however, when Upper Clyde Shipbuilders began to sink beneath the engulfing waves of a financial crisis and when in 1971 giant Rolls-Royce came crashing down. If these traumas had not already sealed the fate of the Government's abortive policy of non-commitment to industry then the crash and near bankruptcy of the Birmingham Small Arms Company in 1973 would almost certainly have done so. Like Rolls-Royce it needed to be picked up and relaunched under the aegis of the state,though in BSA's case it was through a state-aided merger rather than through nationalisation, as with Rolls-Royce.

The Government quickly changed its tune over industrial policy and by 1973 Peter Walker, then Secretary of State for Trade and Industry in the Heath Government, was heralding the dawn of a new age of 'Social Capitalism'. In a lecture given at this time he said:

'As compared both with feudal and with socialist societies, a capitalist society is peculiarly susceptible to lack of moral authority. This is because of its emphasis on freedom and self-dependence and its reliance on rational authority unsupported by religion. This lack of a central moral substance leads only too easily to nihilism.'

In that final sentence he had summed up Britain's industrial malaise all too accurately though he failed to distinguish between the British and the Continental forms of capitalism.

The Old Capitalism

Economic history provides clues to the origin of the present divided state of British industry, a division which manifests itself in one form through the workers' deep-rooted suspicion of shareholders as a class. There was a rush to form joint stock companies in Britain around the time of the great depression of 1874. Limited liability meant that investors could put their money into these companies on the Stock Exchange without too much risk. The trends towards the wider dispersal of industrial equity developed to the point where today there are no less than 3,429* British companies' shares quoted on the Stock Exchange. Dealings in this so-called secondary market when shares change hands totals around £8,540 million* a year and is equivalent to the business done on all the other EEC stock exchanges put together, though only a fraction of this (£276 million)* represents new money going into industry. The rest is simply money passing from one portfolio investor to another.

So, a whole new class of industry owner – the shareholder – came into being in Britain to supersede largely the individual industrial capitalist, who in turn had succeeded the merchant capitalist. To the human 'factor of production' – the worker who hired out his labour – all capitalists came to be regarded as a class apart, even the small shareholder. Attempts to encourage worker participation in industry through wider share ownership have met with very little success, except in the upper echelons of management. The ready availability of industrial equity has encouraged insurance companies, pension funds and other big financial institutions in Britain to channel a great deal of their total savings into this form of investment. These institutions have naturally become major shareholders by consequence, though unlike Continental banks, holding companies and savings institutions they exercise little control over the companies they partly own.

*figures relate to the year 1973.

Fig. 1 *Unilever Limited*

Class of holder

	Number of holdings	Amount of holding £	%
Banks and Discount Companies	5,891	1,377,471	3
Financial Trusts	231	839,320	2
Insurance Companies	757	8,082,825	18
Investment Trusts	384	1,350,139	3
Pension Funds	277	2,003,697	4
Nominee Companies	4,733	7,872,934	17
Other Corporate Holders	1,757	2,139,519	5
	14,030	23,665,905	52
Leverhulme Trust	1	8,443,899	18
Individuals	79,521	13,657,011	30
	93,552	45,766,815	100

Individuals

Holdings of £ £	Number of holdings	Amount of holding £	Average holding £
1- 100	42,804	2,187,645	51
101- 250	23,034	3,824,126	166
251- 500	9,279	3,288,295	354
501- 1,000	3,362	2,300,860	684
1,001- 5,000	1,001	1,631,171	1,630
5,001-10,000	28	185,786	6,635
10,001-25,000	11	159,101	14,464
25,001-50,000	1	29,000	20,000
Over 50,000	1	51,027	51,027
	79,521	13,657,011	

Source: Annual Accounts, 1973.

The diagram shows a fairly typical breakdown of a major quoted British company's shareholders, by class and size of holder.

Elsewhere things developed somewhat differently than in Britain so far as the ownership of industry is concerned. During the period when Britain's long industrial supremacy came to an end, in the latter part of the nineteenth century, it was challenged by Continental nations such as Germany and Belgium as well as by America. Though they started later in the industrial race they were able to profit from Britain's experience, and not simply by paying far more attention as they did to the technical side of production and to the scale of enterprise.

'In industrial finance they devised a method by which permanent capital could be supplied to industry more easily and more cheaply than was the case in England.[6] In both Germany and America most of the permanent capital of industry was supplied by investment banks; in England such capital had to be raised by the issue of shares in the capital market, a method that was not always successful and in any case was slow and costly. The average firm still depended upon undistributed profits for the capital necessary for business expansion. For financial reasons alone the average size of the business unit was much larger in America and Germany than in England.'

Recent studies have shown that the cost of equity capital to British companies still exceeds that of fixed interest borrowings by Continental firms.[7]

The pattern that developed right from the start on the Continent was for investment banks to provide capital direct for industry, though sometimes the banks in turn had to borrow from the public in order to make loans. Often the investment banks would issue the bonds of a particular business enterprise to the public, though they would not part with equity in that business. Such was the case for instance with the Société Générale de Belgique in the financing of the Belgian railways. Where equity was issued it would often be in the holding company rather than in its individual holdings, so the ownership of industry tended to be far less diluted than in Britain and has remained so to the present day.

Those holding companies that do exist in Britain tend to be industrial conglomerates or financial groups making profits from dealing in the shares of their subsidiaries and supplying financial services to them. Elsewhere in Europe they tend to be industrial groups with a banking base (though the two may be legally separate) which specialise in deploying funds and management throughout the group.

It is arguable that, though workers have no control over finished production in any form of modern capitalism, working class animosity against their financial masters can be more acute if they are middle-class shareholders than if they were banks or holding companies.* The very anonymity of many of the Continental shareholding institutions and their lack of a personified identity protects them from such resentment. To many British workers the fact that they are themselves shareholders in industry at one remove, through pension funds or insurance companies, appears irrelevant. The feeling of 'us' and 'them' remains all pervasive and state ownership of industry can appear a more equitable prospect if it means doing 'them' down. 'They' are the people who take the profits out of the company at 'our' expense.

Peter Walker spoke of 'creating a genuine partnership between government, banking and both sides of industry.' It could even now be rather too late for such reforms: many people would regard them as mere tinkering with the system. The Labour Party is committed to a much wider degree of state ownership and though it is probably true, as Peter Walker says, that state ownership has failed to provide people with a sense of participation such truths can easily be pushed aside by pressures for swingeing reform.

The Merger Boom

How has all this affected the structure, as distinct from the psychology, of British industry? The answer is to be seen partly in the rash of take-overs and mergers which has transformed certain sectors during the past decade. Nothing can have drawn attention more sharply to industry in Britain (certainly not its competitive performance in world markets) than this furious rush to put companies together or to break them up. Industrialists and financiers have vied with one another in a scramble to increase the size of their empires and to outbid one another in the price paid for doing so. Terms like 'industrial logic' and 'synergy' have been bandied about freely as a rather specious justification for merging once rival concerns. The most obnoxious breed of contemporary financial/industrial operator, the asset strippers, have not

---

*The Labour Research Department pamphlet on GEC, published after the merger with AEI says of the enhanced value of the combined group, 'all the increase in value goes to the shareholders and none to the workers'. It then goes on to attack the increase in value which the small shareholder (of 100 shares) has seen in his investment.

even troubled to justify their actions in this way. They have simply bought control of industrial enterprises through the stock market in order to close down part of the operation and sell off its assets, usually property, for capital gains, making thousands of workers redundant in the process. Pressed for a justification of his actions the 'stripper' would typically claim to be eliminating inefficient operations and assets in order to redeploy the capital more efficiently elsewhere. In fact the sums realised were generally used to buy up even more unsuspecting concerns and to repeat the operation. A flexible and highly liquid share market eased their path for them. It is only recently that the government, through the Monopolies Commission, has begun to adopt a more searching inquiry into all the consequences of a projected merger, including some of the social ones. The term 'unacceptable face of capitalism' was coined by Mr Heath, the Prime Minister in 1973, to describe what he saw as a specific abuse, but it could be applied fairly to the wave of indiscriminate takeover and merger activity in British business in recent years.

On the Continent, where takeovers are the discreetly conducted exception rather than the rule they have become in Britain and are usually made on a group to group or family to family basis, industrialists have watched the pattern of events in Britain with understandable distaste. Far from wanting to emulate the British system of wider share ownership the governments and financial communities in other European countries have resolved to avoid it at all costs if it means a free-for-all. They have shown a distinct preference for retaining their *dirigiste* systems of control and central direction. Trade unions and British workers generally have been no more enamoured of the system either. Mistrust and suspicion have been engendered and have manifested themselves in demonstrations, sit-ins, the sporadic formation of workers' co-operatives (such as the one formed after the BSA collapse) and, inevitably, calls for the wholesale nationalisation of the means of production.

It is difficult to quantify the degree of industrial change that has taken place during the merger boom, though one survey showed that,[8] of the 2,126 manufacturing firms (outside the steel industry) that were quoted on the U.K. stock exchanges in 1954 more than 400 or close on one-fifth had been taken-over six years later. The number will have increased substantially in the intervening years. It is even more difficult to quantify what benefits, if any, the furious round of takeover and merger activity has brought in its train, though Professor Newbould took the view that the benefits had often been overstated.[9] Since the monopolies and mergers legislation was tightened in 1973 a number of proposed bids by one company for another have been dropped in the face of an official investigation. The suspicion must be that the arguments for the bid would not have stood up to scrutiny. Claims about the advantages of large scale enterprise are particularly vulnerable in this respect, though already the takeover jamboree has claimed a good many casualties in the cause of bigness.

What is abundantly clear is that the take-over boom — it has become an industry in itself for the merchant banks advising the bidders and defenders — is part and parcel of the British capital market system and its historical development. The wide dispersal of industrial equity referred to earlier has made it simple for one business to acquire a substantial proportion of another's shares in the stock market, and then to launch an open bid for the remainder. A Takeover Panel, set up under the aegis of the Bank of England, to curb the worst excesses prevents buying of control in the market but does not prevent a near controlling stake being bought in that way. Shareholders of the company being bid for of course have the right to decline the open bid that follows market buying by a bidder, but in practice the temptation to accept an offer (particularly where it is in cash and where increased dividend income is promised) has proved to be powerful. Questions of whether or not the bid is good for the future management of their company can easily be overlooked by small shareholders in such cases. Only in a few cases have they stood loyally by their companies and fended off a bid* which they did not feel to be in its best interests.

The sums offered by one company wanting to take over another have often been bid up to astronomic heights. The biggest so far was the £350 million bid by Grand Metropolitan Hotels group for Watney Mann the brewers. The fact that such bids are rarely in cash but in the 'paper' (shares or loan stock) of the acquiring company or a mixture of cash and paper, is something that has escaped the appreciation of many workers. They have simply seen vast sums of money apparently changing hands and this has tended to fuel their own inflationary demands for wage increases.

Virtually every sector of British industry has been affected to greater or lesser extent by the takeover boom, though some have been far more drastically re-shaped than others. The electrical equipment industry,

---

*The United Drapery Stores unsuccessful bid for Debenhams, the department store group was a case in point.

motor vehicles, breweries, hotels, textile,* catering and the retail sectors have been among the principal targets of the bidders.

The 'Professionals'

Probably the best-known name in this connection is Sir Arnold Weinstock. Many foreigners as well as British people will mention him first if asked to name a prominent British industrialist. This is interesting because it shows how the lineal barons of industry in Britain, men such as Lord Pilkington for instance, have sunk into relative obscurity so far as popular image is concerned. Yet Weinstock founded no new enterprise as the older industrial entrepreneurs did but built his electrical empire (the General Electric Company) to its present size through rising to the top of an existing company which he then used as a vehicle to take over rivals in the electrical industry.

Until 1967, practically no-one had heard of Weinstock. His origins are relatively obscure. The London-born son of a Polish tailor who graduated in statistics, he joined a small radio and television manufacturing company called Sobell which was subsequently taken over by GEC in 1961. He was taken onto the main board and, when the company was 'facing ruin', as he puts it, he was elected the man to save it and made managing director. His technique was incisive: sharp cuts in costs, the size of the operation and in the work force. It was a technique which was to become the *modus operandi* of a spectacular career.

By 1967 GEC was so far recovered as to be able to launch a takeover bid for Associated Electrical Industries (AEI), an old business empire run by men of the *ancien régime* and apparently unable to survive the abrasive cut and thrust of modern commerce, though its engineering was generally acknowledged to be sound. A rival bid from General Electric of America (no connection with GEC) was rumoured at the time. To what extent this was a deliberate bogy raised to scare AEI and the country at large has never been quite clear but AEI succumbed to the GEC bid. Another major heavy electrical manufacturer, English

---

*Textiles provide a very good illustration of the point. In 1969 the (Labour) Government, because of the degree of nationalisation that had already taken place in the industry, banned any further links between Courtaulds, English Calico, Viyella, Carrington and Dewhurst and Coats Patons. Yet by 1974 Carrington and Dewhurst and Viyella had merged to form Carrington-Viyella, which is now a subsidiary of ICI.

Electric, followed suit shortly afterwards and became part of GEC.

Both GEC and English Electric were publicly quoted companies but they could hardly expect to call on their shareholders, many of which were small shareholders, to subscribe rights issues to carry the companies through times of poor profit or even loss. Rights issues go down well with the stock market only when a company's fortunes are at a high point and the promise of a good return on the shareholders' new money is strong. A Belgian banker-industrialist commenting on the GEC/AEI/English Electric affair suggested that both companies would have stood a better chance of survival under the Belgian holding company system (see page 111).

Whether this would simply have meant perpetuating inefficient management is a moot point but the Weinstock solution was not to maintain AEI and EE by the injection of fresh management but to merge them fully with GEC and to cut back their operations drastically. Many thousands of redundancies were created in the process.*

Weinstock is undeniably a very capable business man. He has created a powerful and profitable enterprise in the new GEC and earned himself a very good reputation with its shareholders in the process. But his critics would say that by amputating many of the heavy engineering limbs of the companies he took over, and grafting only the most profitable parts onto the corporate body of GEC he has lost certain engineering capacity to the nation, and that the activities he preserved could hardly have failed to make a good profit.

Donald Stokes (Lord Stokes as he is now) achieved prominence around the same time as Weinstock and for reasons that were not dissimilar. His business empire, British Leyland is very much a product of the takeover and merger boom. Like Weinstock, Stokes is no industrial entrepreneur. He joined the Leyland Motors commercial vehicle group in 1930 as a student engineering apprentice and worked his way up to become chairman and managing director. In 1968 – year of the supermerger in Britain – Leyland merged with British Motor Holdings and British Leyland was born with Stokes at its head. British Motor Holdings was itself very much a merger product. Austin and Morris came together in 1952 to form the British Motor Corporation and later became BMH on the addition of Jaguar. Leyland for its part had taken over Standard-Triumph in 1961 and Rover in 1967. So, the

*In the four years from 1969 to 1971 the GEC group reduced its workforce by 36,00 – from 206,000 to 17,000 according to the Labour Research Department.

1968 merger of Leyland and BMH wedded just about all the non-American automobile makers in Britain but was certainly 'no love match' as Lord Stokes himself conceded afterwards.

British Leyland was nowhere near so ruthless in its redundancy policy after the supermerger as GEC had been. But one factor which must have led Stokes to avoid closures on the Weinstock model was the fear of provoking a large-scale strike throughout the group. As things are, British Leyland has been beset by almost constant labour troubles since its formation and only very recently has the situation begun to come under some sort of control. Stokes is determined to forge a successful new, European-scale entity out of British Leyland though it remains to be seen whether he can do it. Apart from the labour troubles, profits performance has been disappointing (for which the share price has suffered and the group had to have very substantial cash injections of state loans, since repaid) and British Leyland's position among world motor companies has slipped badly in the years since its formation.

Right from the outset in 1968, Lord Stokes argued that it would take at least five years to forge the separate elements of the British Leyland group into a successful single entity and to reap the economies of scale. He has been repeatedly critical of the City (the Stock Exchange in effect) for not being prepared to take an equally long-term view of British Leyland as an investment. Because of its extremely low share price the group is at a considerable disadvantage when it requires to raise new money through rights issues to its shareholders. Lord Kearton, head of Courtaulds, Britain's biggest textiles group, has attacked the City much more vehemently on similar grounds, claiming that it was too short-sighted to support the rationalisation and re-equipping of the ailing textile industry which he was trying to bring about. Typically the City has countered that it judged performance by profits and that this is the only true yardstick in a capitalist society. However an increasing number of British industrialists seem to share the Stokes/Kearton view to a greater or lesser extent.

If a drive for economies of scale production has imposed a rather stark uniformity on some of British Leyland's motorcars this is also a characteristic of many other aspects of British business since the merger boom. Hotels, public houses and beers are indicative of the trend, and Maxwell Joseph is a prime symbol of it. He is the man behind Grand Metropolitan Hotels, which in a concerted bout of super concentration took over Watney Mann the brewer, adding it to Trumans, another brewery it already owned, and gobbled up Mecca, Berni Inns as well as numerous hotel chains. One of the few London hotels to escape the takeover boom is the world famous Savoy which was able to defend itself only through a device which looks likely to be denied to companies by law in future. This is the issue of shares with no votes, or relatively few votes, to the wide public while the original owners of the business hold onto control with the voting shares.

Jim Slater is a unique phenomenon on the modern business scene, or he was at least, until other financial operators in Britain began to copy and cramp his style. Yet while Slater's name is almost universally known, his activities within Slater Walker, the financial empire he built up with none other than Peter Walker, have always been rather ill-understood by people outside the international financial community. Is Slater Walker a bank, a holding company or what? The answer is that in some ways it is both, yet in other ways neither: it is a special sort of animal which has thrived in the climate of the British capital market. It is only a holding company in a very limited sense in the Continental meaning of being a nurturing parent for its subsidiaries. It does have industrial subsidiaries and does provide them with funds, but equally it takes profits for providing these services and an even greater profit from dealing in the shares of the business offsprings it spawns. Perhaps Slater Walker is best likened in some respects to a vast warehouse for storing shareholdings it has built up in various key financial enterprises over a number of years. These strategic stakes can be used for putting companies together behind the scenes,which means dealing profits, or for passing onto another company which wants a ready-made parcel of shares prior to making a bid inthe stock market for the rest. In July 1973 it was revealed that Slater Walker owned more than 10 per cent of no fewer than forty-five leading British companies. The general practice of 'warehousing' shares has become an undesirable activity so far as both major political parties are concerned and the 1973 Finance Bill proposed public disclosure of any shareholding above 5 per cent of a company's total equity.

The secret of men like Slater has been to convince the stock market of their virtual infallibility. Success then became a sort of self-fulfilling prophecy: the more the financial operating companies could boost their image and their share price, the more companies they could take over using those shares for payment and thus boost their profits and assets even more. Stock market credulity was stretched beyond its limits by some of the operators however, (though this does not apply to Slater) and share prices declined, making some of the financial empires look dangerously like houses of cards. Even Slater

Walker has begun to contract some of its international operations of late, such as those in the Far East where stock markets took a very nasty tumble in 1973.

Slater Walker's universal philosophy, to quote Jim Slater, is that 'we are money makers, not thing makers'. The extent to which the money makers have seized the limelight from the thing makers in British industry in recent years prompted *The Times* to comment: 'The old generation of thing makers is dead; long live the architects of the new financial revolution.'[10] The impression has become one of a society of financiers rather than of great industrial entrepreneurs.

Yet the dedicated thing makers are not quite dead. Their philosophy is perhaps best summed up by Lord Pilkington, head of Pilkington Brothers the glassmakers. 'We have never been interested in making money for its own sake,' he said. It is the very antithesis of the Slater creed.

Dynasties in Decline?

For almost a century and a half Pilkingtons have dominated the British glassmaking industry, just as they have dominated the life of St. Helens in Lancashire — their 'company town' and one of the few left in Britain now. Until 1970, Pilkingtons had financed themselves without any outside equity for nearly fifty years and even managed to finance their now world famous float-glass process from internal resources and borrowings. Then in 1970, the glass giant went public for the inevitable reason that the family were becoming too dependent upon the business and needed to realise some of their assets. In Europe Pilkingtons might well have gone to an investment bank, just as the French glassmaker, Saint-Gobain-Pont-à-Mousson, sold a large slice of its equity to the Compagnie Financière de Suez. In Britain the tradition is to go to the stock market to sell shares and not to a bank except where the company is very new and small and can persuade a specialised merchant bank or similar institution to hold its shares. There has been little or no effect yet on the way Pilkingtons is run. Lord Pilkington says that an era does not end quite so quickly after a four-generations rule by the same family. Nevertheless, going public can sometimes be the start of the slippery slope towards ultimate loss of control and of the business itself if there is a takeover bidder waiting in the wings.

Lord Pilkington dislikes the term 'company town', just as he is wary of admitting to being a paternalist. 'Paternalism is a dirty word — at the moment,' he says. It was not always so and may not always be so regarded.

'If paternalism means deliberately taking away all power of decision from an individual on the grounds that we know what is best for him, then we are not paternalistic. If it means that we really have tried to have an interest in and care for the future of our employees then I would not quarrel with the term being applied to us. You do not want to sap people's potential by fathering them but ultimately you are responsible for them.'

Pilkingtons had to go public. 'We had grown too big and too vulnerable,' Lord Pilkington says, 'Too many people were wanting to reduce their dependence upon us. Many of us, including myself, had all our money wrapped up in the business.' But he made the point that the company might not have been able to develop the all-important float-glass process had it gone public earlier. It was one thing to gamble with the family money: quite another to risk the funds of the shareholders at large.

When Pilkingtons went public its name disappeared from the rolls of a little-known organisation called the Unquoted Companies Group. It is little known largely because it does not publicise its activities to the general public and partly because public interest centres on the Stock Exchange. Yet no fewer than 98 per cent of British companies are unquoted.* Many of these are 'public' companies but it is possible to be a public company without having a stock market quotation or listing.

Britain's industrial structure can be likened to a pyramid (see Fig. 2). The apex is made up of the quoted companies where such industrial giants as Shell, British Petroleum, Imperial Chemical Industries, Unilever and British-American-Tobacco dominate the landscape. The base consists of the myriad much smaller private companies. But there are some very large industrial and service groups in the middle which are not quoted on the Stock Exchange yet whose sales, typically of between £50 million and £100 million a year, greatly outstrip those of the smaller quoted companies. This narrow band on the pyramid covers

*There are 300,000 active unquoted companies and 9,000 active quoted companies in the United Kingdom. These figures exclude financial companies and nationalised corporations. Out of the 300,000 unquoted companies, Dun & Bradstreet state that there are 42,500 significant companies with a sales average of over £500,000 a year. Disregarding government employees, 51 per cent of employment is in the unquoted sector and 49 per cent in the quoted company sector.

Fig. 2 The Position of the Large Private Company

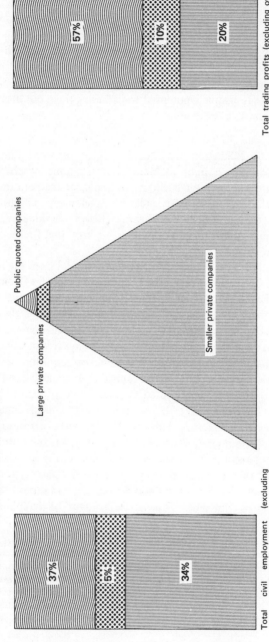

Public quoted companies

Large private companies

Smaller private companies

57%

10%

20%

Total trading profits (excluding overseas owned and controlled companies and nationalised industries).

37%

5%

34%

Total civil employment (excluding nationalised industries and government and government employment).

Source: The Private Company Today. A.J. Merrett and M.E. Lehr; Gower Press.

only one-and-half per cent of its total area[11] yet it embraces some very powerful groups.

Many of them are members of the Unquoted Companies Group. It was formed by Emmanuel Kaye, an industrial entrepreneur, to lobby in the cause of the unquoted company and broadly speaking to help this type of company stave off what Kaye would see as the evil day when it has to go and sell itself on the stock market. Its ranks however have been rather sadly depleted in recent times as, one by one, some great family companies have proved unequal to the financial struggle of remaining independent and have sold out to the public.

Until this happened (over the past two or three years) it would have been hard to find a greater concentration of business power in Britain than at one of the meetings of the Unquoted Companies Group. It would have been possible to see ranged around the table men like Evelyn de Rothschild of bankers Rothschild, Lord Pilkington, Maurice MacMillan of publishers MacMillan, Sir Robert Sainsbury of Sainsbury supermarkets, Sir David Brown of the David Brown organisation, Sir Edwin McAlpine of Sir Robert McAlpine construction, Sebastian de Ferranti of Ferranti the electronics group and Sir Alfred Owen of Rubery Owen the Midlands engineers. Since 1970 however, the Pilkingtons, Sainsburys and McAlpines have all obtained stock market quotations, Ferrantis are expecting to do so and Mr MacMillan left to join the Conservative Government after 1970. Others have taken their place on the UCG but it may be only a matter of time before they pass from the ranks of the unquoted companies too.

The trend saddens Kaye. He is a stern defender of the private company faith. 'We all feel we can make a better contribution to the national economy and do a better job industrially as unquoted companies,' he says in justification of his independent stand against the tide of public quotations. 'Industrialists must be free from the constant threat of takeover if they are to function effectively.'* Once quoted, a company becomes obsessed with short-term profitability and with its share price in order to fend off prospective bidders or to make sure the value of its own bidding currency is high. Kaye says that quoted

---

*'..... the private companies, being free from the danger of being taken over, are the ones that are able to take really long views and to invest in the distant future without the need to consider an immediate profit. This is a real point, and something where they have a great advantage over any but the very largest of all public companies.' (Lord Pilkington).

companies spend too much time looking over their shoulder instead of looking forward.

If Kaye is to be believed, the quoted company lists are full of industrialists who have gone to the stock market then later regretted it when they found themselves no longer free to act in the company's best long-term interests. They find that they have to cut down on capital investment and on research and development so that they can maximise profits and dividends in the interests of keeping up their share price. Kaye thinks this 'short sighted sort of attitude' must have some overall bearing on the performance of British industry. He quotes the recent plight of the U.K. machine tool industry which is comprised mainly of quoted companies. They went on paying out dividends when they should have been investing to beat competition, competition coming largely from West Germany where the industry is mainly in private hands and more concerned with capital investment than with paying dividends.

This view is substantiated by official statistics.* Meanwhile Kaye's own company Lansing Bagnall of which he is 'governing director' (a rare title in Britain, denoting absolute control) has never paid a dividend on its ordinary shares. In the space of seventeen years it has grown from a bankrupt seven-man firm to become Britain's biggest fork lift truck maker with sales of more than £40 million a year and employing some 5,000 people. Kaye leaves no doubt in anyone's mind that as he sees, number one public enemy is not so much the trade unions, as the stock market operator – the whole breed of speculative bidders, asset strippers and dealers.

The reason why so many companies have gone public in recent times and thus helped change the structure of British industry is that inflation has greatly enlarged the cost of financing business. The clearing banks have traditionally been prepared to advance several hundreds of

---

*The September 1968 issue of Incomes, Prices, Employment and Production (one of the last to give the breakdown) issued by the Department of Employment and Productivity compared 133 quoted companies and 263 unquoted ones in the metal and engineering sectors. Both groups had total sources of funds (profit plus depreciation, short-term credit and capital issues) of £311 million in total. From these funds the unquoted companies invested 67½ per cent more in fixed assets than the quoted ones. Quoted companies on the other hand spent 133 per cent more in dividends. The quoted companies made a return of 12.2 per cent on shareholders' funds whereas the unquoted companies rate of return was 14.4 per cent, the inference being that unquoted companies make the most efficient use of capital.

thousands of pounds on overdraft but not several millions, whereas this is the size of sum industry is looking for. In the City of London industrialists have been told by the merchant bankers that they can have the money but only if they are prepared to part with shares in the business in return. Unlike the Continental 'banque d'affaires', however, the merchant banks are generally reluctant to act as investment bankson any major scale and to hold on to equityfor their clients. They want an 'out' from their holding and they persuade the industrialist to seek a full public quotation in order to provide this means of exit.

The proprietor's family in a private company will usually want an easy way out of the holding they are locked into. The problem can become acute when a great industrial family such as the Pilkingtons reaches the fourth generation. By this stage there can be several hundred near and distant relatives of the original proprietor's heir whose fortunes are all tied up in the family business.

As David Owen, the acting chairman of Rubery Owen says, no-one would want to avoid begetting children simply to avoid family problems in the shareholding of a company. Yet the bigger the proprietor's ultimate family becomes the greater becomes the strain upon it as a business entity. There is always the expedient of paying large dividends to the family shareholders, though these are taxed at high, unearned income rates. It is a very costlyway of dissipating assets: it is better to keep them in the company and to build it up.

The Owens, too, have faced big problems of death duties since the death of Ernest Owen, brother of Sir Alfred, who has himself been rather seriously ill since his stroke in1969. However, the Owens have no immediate intention of going to the stock market and in fact a stock market quotation is not such a popular way of anticipating death duties among private companies as is commonly supposed in Britain. A quotation has been seen actually to increase the incidence of death duties in some instances and increasingly industrialists see the point that it is worth waiting until after a family death or a series of them before making a move to go public. This way they may get a more conservative valuation of their company's worth by the revenue authorities than the stock market would have decided upon. Sometimes companies go public thereafter to meet the duties, or even negotiate a straight sale of the business to someone else.

Sir Alfred Owen was *pater familias* to the 13,000 Rubery Owen employees while he was active as chairman and his son David inevitably continues the paternalistic tradition to some extent. He has to live with his father's public pronouncement that 'people matter more than profits' and as a result he usually takes the longer, more humane and more costly route towards cutting costs and rationalising the family business empire. This shows up in the profit and loss account, too, but a Weinstock-style approach of 'taking the knife' to the business can hardly be adopted when the chief executive is also the principal owner of the business. On the credit side, labour relations have been generally good at Rubery Owens and its products (it is a leading supplier to the motor industry) are well regarded.

Sebastian de Ferranti who, with his brother Basil, runs Ferranti Limited has little time for financiers and people who 'move paper money about in the City' while, as he sees things, engineers increase the real wealth of the nation. He and his brother are engineers as were their father and grandfather before them. Grandfather Ferranti was the man who pioneered the high voltage AC electricity generating and transmission systems which were widely adopted throughout the world. He 'got it right' unlike Edison who promoted the low voltage local DC systems in America, says Sebastian. But Edison was a 'financial Johnny' where Grandfather Ferranti was engineer. The Ferrantis are true 'thing makers'.

If Ferrantis had been a quoted public company they might well have found it hard going persuading shareholders to finance the initial cost of micro-circuit development – an area where the company has held onto about the only British stake. It costs around £10 million to join the micro-circuit 'club'. Only part of this investment has yet paid off but Ferrantis are confident it all will in time. In the meantime Sebastian does not let the outsider miss the point that it was his family company which kept the British stake in this high technology sector while Arnold Weinstock took GEC out of microcircuits.

Sebastian de Ferranti maintains that one of the virtues of truly private, private enterprise is that it can take this sort of long-term view. Another is that family proprietors like he and his brother have little fear of being elbowed out by other people as are the directors in a quoted company, where they can be voted in and out of office by shareholder factions. Therefore, the owner-directors can afford to encourage bright people instead of suppressing them. Ferrantis are in fact considering a Stock Exchange listing as (through a family rupture in the past) some 40 per cent of the shares are already held outside the family. Sebastian is confident that he and his brother, who jointly have control of the company, could always fight off an unwanted takeover bid. The City takes a different view however. It holds that if a takeover bid is fair and generous to the outside shareholders, family directors should be prepared to let them take advantage of it. It is in this way that many directors have been pressed into relinquishing control of their companies.

The trend towards wider ownership of companies can occasionally be reversed as Sir David Brown, head of the David Brown engineering concern, has proved. Following a financial crisis in the company and the sale of subsidiaries like Aston Martin and Lagonda cars as well as of David Brown Tractors, Sir David restored absolute control by buying back in the quoted preference shares. He claims that his managerial style was cramped by allowing in outside professional executives and that now his is a very private, private company again he no longer has to play politics as so often happens in a public company. The David Brown organisation has prospered since. Sir David is also the controlling shareholder in Vosper-Thorneycroft the shipbuilders which he likes to term 'our public sector'.

Some of the best-run companies in Britain are among those which only very recently have been forced to leave the ranks of the unquoted. The highly nepotistic giant holding company, S. Pearson & Son is a case in point. Presided over by Lord Cowdray the group embraces such diverse interests as Lazard Brothers the merchant bank, the Financial Times and Westminster Press and Allied English Potteries (through the Standard Industrial group). Lord Poole, former chairman of the Conservative Party is among its directors and many of the key posts are filled by Lord Cowdray's relatives or friends. Lord Cowdray (the first Viscount was Weetman Dickinson Pearson, a Yorkshire contractor) is a classic, almost caricature, English aristocratic figure. He is a leading landowner, an authority on forestry and salmon and Who's Who lists his prime interests as hunting, shooting and fishing as well as polo playing. He has been described as a true aristocrat but one with a drive to make money. Despite all the nepotism and family domination, S. Pearson is run with 'flair and efficiency'.[1 2] One senses that it only grudgingly let the public into its shareholding and that because of impending death duty problems.

The construction industry remained just about a total stronghold of private companies until the Sir Robert McAlpine interests went public as 'Newarthill' in 1972. Sir Robin McAlpine, the present chairman, had been quoted before as saying he would 'hate every minute' of going public. Families remain very powerful in the industry however. Neil Wates (a member of the Unquoted Companies Group) is head of the family building empire. Sir Godfrey Mitchell, his family and trusts control more than half the voting shares in George Wimpey and the

Laing family hold 80 per cent of John Laing either directly or indirectly. Sir Maurice Laing has a theory about why families so dominate: 'To run a successful contracting organisation it is essential for the top men to be entrepreneurs and this calls for an authoritarian type of manager who does not like being bossed around even by his own shareholders.'[13]

Guarding the Guardians

The reluctance displayed by many companies towards going public and the outright suspicion that some industrialists have of the Stock Exchange argues against a convenient myth in the City of London. This conjures up the caricature of the German banker, the French bureaucrat or the functionary of the Italian state cracking the whip over hapless industrialists who look on with envy at the freedom of the British industrialist. The extension of this myth is that it can only be a matter of time before Continentals see the light and come over to the British system.

Fortunately this delusion is not universal. Successive governors of the Bank of England have recently tried to persuade the most respectable and powerful of the City's financial institutions such as insurance companies, pension funds and unit trusts to take a more active interest in the companies where they are often the largest single shareholder. So far these attempts have met with little success. The institutions hold fast to the idea that their business is investment and not industry. The rather negative general view seems to be that if a company fails to perform well they have the ultimate sanction against it of disposing of their shareholding. Arguably it is their passiveness on this issue which gave free rein to the operations of less desirable elements in the City and on the Stock Exchange in particular.

Increasingly there is a view that the clearing banks will have to grasp the nettle of maintaining shareholdings in industry and helping to monitor or improve its performance. They will have to abandon their traditional rôle as providers of overdraft and short-term finance in favour of long-term investment in industry. As Readman says: 'British banking seems to be moving towards the Continental pattern of department store banks with clearing banks taking on merchant banking functions'.[6]

'The difference between Continental and British bank involvement in industry is probably of even greater importance. We have seen how German banks and Belgian and Italian holding companies dominate industry. In France the banques d'affaires and the Caisse de Dépots have large interests and the clearing banks are increasing their participations through their merchant banking subsidiaries. Like the American banks these employ industrial experts and have the capacity to intervene in the management of companies in which they have large participations.'

Things may go a rather different way however, if the Labour Party is able to proceed with its plans for much greater state involvement in industry. Wherever direct aid is given to a company from public funds a Labour government will reserve the right to take a share of the ownership. It is intended that in this way, shipbuilding and repairing and the aero-space industry as well possibly as North Sea oil exploitation shall be taken into public ownership. The aero-engine division of Rolls-Royce is already in state ownership within the nationalised Rolls-Royce (1971) company formed after RR went bankrupt in 1971. State holdings will also be sought by a Labour government in construction, machine tools, road haulage and pharmaceuticals.

The idea is that a new National Enterprise Board should establish control through equity holdings over the one hundred or so largest companies in Britain, which would have to surrender shares in return for state assistance. The board would be a parastatal body rather like the IRI or ENI in Italy (see p.47). It would be hardly surprising to see nominees of this new super holding company on the boards of companies where it held stakes. The formula seems to have worked well enough in Italy and might work in Britain though the sheer size and diversity of the NEB might work against it. The formula of total nationalisation applied in the past to coal, gas, electricity, railways and steel is now thought by many in the Labour Party to be too drastic a means of extending state ownership even if total ownership of the means of production remains the goal of many others in the Party.

There is always the danger that in the clash of ideologies between the Conservative and Labour Parties over the ownership of industry, the compromise of sensible reforms in the present system is not tried. Probably what is most needed is an orderly system of ensuring the growth of industrial companies after they reach the size where family ownership is no longer practicable. All but the biggest quoted groups need protection too from arbitrary takeover. Either the banks or holding companies could fulfil this rôle by supplying finance in return for equity stakes and by holding on to them. Inevitably this would mean some decline in the importance of the Stock Exchange but it is arguable that otherwise the stock market will bring about its own downfall anyway.

Restructuring the ownership of British industry in this way might also dissipate some of the shop-floor animosity towards shareholders and even towards management, if managers were no longer thought to be the tools of a shareholder's bourgeoisie. It would almost certainly go more to the heart of the problem than the rather nebulous proposal from the Liberal Party that there should be 'shareholder members and employee members of a company' and the equally ineffective proposition from various quarters, including the Conservative Party that employee 'participation' be encouraged through works councils. Only the Labour Party seems to have a positive policy towards industry ownership, albeit an unwieldy and bureaucratic one. This policy could well be implemented by default if the Conservative and Liberal Parties do not agree to some fairly fundamental reforms of the present system.

Freedom in Size

Perhaps rather little has been said in all this about many of the great quoted public companies in Britain which dominate the fundamental industry sectors such as oils, chemicals, engineering, papermaking and so on (most steel production is in the hands of the nationalised British Steel Corporation). Typically they will be owned by an (unco-ordinated) alliance of investment institutions and small shareholders with the founding family (if it is still there at all) and the directors having only a tiny share of the company's equity. Thus they are highly vulnerable to outside takeover. An example of how easily the fate of even the biggest industrial giant can be manipulated by outside financial interests (and one which shocked even the City) was that of the link engineered by Jim Slater between Bowater, world's biggest newsprint producer and Ralli the commodity group. Before the merger Slater's old rival, Nigel Broackes of Trafalgar House Investments (which incidentally took over Cunard during its conglomerate empire building) made a bid himself for Bowater on condition that it dropped its bid for Ralli. The fact that the fate of an industrial giant like Bowater could be so easily manipulated awed even the more hardened of City operators.

Paradoxically among the most effective of British industrial companies in recent years are those which have adopted a low public profile and which by virtue of sheer size have been spared the much vaunted benefits or 'synergy' and 'rationalisation' via merger.

CHAPTER 6   THE NETHERLANDS: THE SECRET '200'
Sue Masterman & Anton Koene

'Secrecy runs in the Dutch blood, just as it does with the Chinese' (Rudi Vrom, head of Vrom and Dreesman, in a newspaper interview).

The barons of Dutch industry are in the main anonymous and hard working businessmen. They are grey figures who are never featured in the international gossip columns because they rarely have time to do anything which would cause international comment. Their private lives are outwardly impeccable, certainly while they are in Holland. They fear God and worship Mammon, and work with an intensity and panache which has put Dutch industry at the top of the charts internationally.

In October 1968 Piet Mertens, the chairman of the *Nederlandse Katholiek Vakverbond (NKV)*, one of the three main trade union organisations in the Netherlands, formulated the trade unions' main problem – the difficulty of identifying the grey men who hold the power. He posed the hypothesis that Dutch industry was in the hands of around 200 individuals – industrialists, bankers, ex-ministers and government officials with a high degree of inter-relation through family and industrial ties. 'Mertens 200' unleashed a whole series of investigations into the identity of the group, but up to the present time no one is much wiser. The barons have surrounded themselves with a seemingly impregnable defence system and by exerting pressure through a system which could be called moral industrial disarmament have kept the curious, whether unions or shareholders, at bay. Piet Mertens is now Secretary of State for Social Affairs, and in line for a place in the ranks of this élite.

Religio-political Influences

The Industrial Revolution came late to Holland, right at the end of the nineteenth century. Until then the Netherlands had been a basically agricultural society, outside the vital trading activities which had historically attracted banking and insurance to the country. The founders of Dutch industry were the enterprising families who dared to go it alone. Today their third or fourth generations are still the owners of the majority of the small- and medium-sized Dutch industries, and a large proportion of privately controlled major Dutch concerns. There are, however, different patterns of family influence in the running of the various groups. To understand the pattern of power it is necessary, briefly and simply, to take a look at the historical roots and the social background of these families.

The Reformation border runs straight across the Netherlands, dividing it roughly into a Protestant north, and a Roman Catholic south, with a relatively recent group of those who are religiously disinterested concentrated in the densely-populated west of the country. Each of these groups claim roughly one-third of the population of 13.5 million. The Dutch present a united front to the world outside their borders, but within the Netherlands the competition and rivalry between the Protestant and the Roman Catholic sectors still smoulders.

The Dutch Constitution guarantees religious freedom to all; the effect on Dutch society of this religious division is fundamental. There are three main trade union organisations, the Roman Catholic, the Protestant and the Socialist. The Socialists and the Roman Catholics are now federated – the Socialists outnumber the other two in membership. The Protestant union is prepared to federate, but it retains a hard core of members who refuse to strike on biblical grounds. It says much for Dutch tolerance that pay awards achieved after strike action, in which the Protestants have refused to take part, are given to all employees. What would be seen as black-legging in other countries is regarded as normal.

The *zuilen* system – society based on the pillars of various beliefs and ideologies – tends to perpetuate itself since the education system is also split up into Protestant, Roman Catholic and 'public' groups. This promotes the isolation of these groups outside the big cities, and intensifies the isolation in the academic world among both university and school staff.

In the world of communication the *zuilen* system is most obvious. Two TV channels and three radio stations have their time split up between one national broadcasting organisation (NOS), two without ideological basis (AVRO and TROS), one socialist (VARA), one Roman Catholic (KRO), two Protestant (NCRV and EO) and one former Protestant organisation which has defrocked itself (VPRO). The Press is equally divided, with the result that there is a proliferation of small-circulation intellectual and quasi-intellectual publications, and no popular Press at all in the sense of a British *Daily Mirror* or a West German *Bild Zeitung*. The provincial Press plays an influential rôle, and naturally reflects the predominant opinion or belief in the area which it covers.

This multiplicity in the Press is reflected in Parliament and, as we shall see, in industry. The Netherlands enjoys an incredible scale of political parties, of whom up to twenty compete in general elections; the number in Parliament varying between thirteen and fifteen as splinter parties come and go. Post-war Dutch governments have all been coalitions. Leaving aside the fanatical religious parties and the farmers' party on the Right, and the pacificists and the Communists on the left, power in the Dutch Parliament is left in the hands of the Socialists (*Partij van de Arbeid*) with the largest parliamentary party, the liberals (*Volkspartij voor Vrijheid en Democratie*), the Roman Catholics (*Katholieke Volkspartij*) and the two major Protestant parties (*Antirevolutionaire Partij* and *Christelijk-Historische Unie*). Three smaller parties, two on the left (*Politieke Partij Radikalen* and *Democraten '66*) and one on the right (*Democratische Socialisten '70*) complete the picture.

The one constant factor in the three, four- and five-party coalition governments between 1948 and 1974 has been the Roman Catholic KVP. The balance of power, however, has shifted slowly towards the left during the last decade. This reflects the trend away from the *zuilen* system and the slow progress towards left, right and centre groups in society and politics. The liberals are the free-traders in Dutch politics, and as such form the hard core on the right. The three major Christian Democratic parties are struggling towards a federation in the *Christen Democratisch Appel* (CDA) with visions of winning a permanent balance of power in the centre. The socialists are rapidly pulling in support from the members of the smaller radical parties, which may be swallowed in the socialist mass. The result of this evolution, rather than revolution, in Dutch politics has been a succession of governments, few of whom have served their full four-year term in office. Politics in the Netherlands is rarely a lifetime career. It is merely a stepping stone which leads either to a position of top Eurocrat or UN function or straight to the boardroom. This applies not only to government politics but also to regional posts, and careers in government advisory bodies. The Netherlands has a prolific supply of ex-premiers, ministers and state secretaries who have, after a relatively short period in office, taken their know-how to posts with better prospects and better pay in industry, commerce and the international civil service.

Examples are not difficult to find. Ex-premier Jelle Zijlstra is chairman of the Netherlands Central Bank. He turned down the offer of a second term in office as premier and retired to a position of power screened off from the outside world, emerging to lecture the Dutch once or twice a year. He turned down the post of president of the IMF because it meant moving his family out of the Netherlands. Jovial in private, austere in public, Zijlstra, one of the sons of a farming family from Friesland, is one of the most powerful men in the Netherlands. An ex-Finance Minister, Hendrik Witteveen, is president of the IMF. Apart from his activities as a leading member of the Sufi movement in the Netherlands he left little impression on the Dutch scene except that of a financial expert.

Ex-ministers of agriculture also play key rôles. Sicco Mansholt was a former president of the EEC commission in Brussels and now continues his rôle behind the scenes. Piet Lardinois, another ex-agricultural minister, is busy career building in Brussels. With Boerema heading the FAO in Rome, and Joseph Luns, Dutch foreign minister for nineteen years, as secretary-general of NATO, the Dutch are well placed internationally. But for every Dutch ex-politician in international public service, there is another running a major industrial company.

Power Anonymous

Many efforts have been made to track down the 'Mertens 200'. These studies all reinforce Mertens' basic hypothesis, that the small group at the top of banking, industry and government is closely and intensively inter-related. Industry makes sure that it picks up the ex-government members who can best serve their purposes.

The only way to find out who is who in Dutch board-rooms is to comb through the annual reports. Yet even this gives a clouded picture, since very many Dutch companies manage to avoid publishing an annual report, or produce one with an absolute minimum of information. Now that the larger companies with the normal N.V. (limited liability) structure have been compelled to publish there has been a panic-stricken rush into the B.V. (closed limited liability) form which gives more room for evasion.

The most secretive figures in Dutch industry are probably the Brenninkmeÿer family, owners and in full control of a concern whose turnover in 1970 was estimated at £700 million ($1,680 million) and who employ around 35,000 people in more than 200 world wide companies better known to the public as C & A. Officially, with the exception of their West German subsidiary where they are legally obliged to publish, there is no information available concerning the results of C & A or the activities of the Brenninkmeÿers. C & A is now controlled by 200 male members of the Brenninkmeÿer family, and the whole hierarchy is imbued with the philosophy that making results public is a sign of weakness.

The Brenninkmeÿers started their first shop in the Netherlands in the 1840s in the small northern provincial town Sneek, after two centuries of traipsing across the country from their German homes to sell linen to wealthy Dutch farmers. The first year's profit was £120 ($290), and the brothers Clement and August, whose initials became the company's hallmark only used £30 ($72) for private expenditure. For very many years the Roman Catholic Brenninkmeÿers kept C & A exclusively a Roman Catholic concern, and although this has now been relaxed Mass is still said before important board meetings. The C & A philosophy is basically that since the firm fulfills all its duties to society, in the form of settling its debts within eight days and creating good social security schemes for its staff, it has no duty to justify its behaviour by publishing facts and figures. Since C & A is one of the largest advertisers in the newspaper world, the Press is discouraged from prying too deeply into their affairs. From their Amsterdam head-quarters this group has a vital influence on the clothing trade in general. They only stock articles specially made for their stores. Although they tend to be less dictatorial to the textile industry than in the past, they can, with 15 per cent of the off-the-peg clothing market in the Netherlands, dictate their terms. The Brenninkmeÿers do not mix their influence directly with that of other firms or banks – unlike the general pattern in the Netherlands. At most there could be some Brenninkmeÿer influence through the marriage of daughters of the family to members of other influential Dutch business families. In their splendid isolation the C & A concern is one of the most successful Dutch international enterprises.

A firm with Protestant roots is Philips Gloeilampen. The Philips family retains control, but has delegated its power to the managers who have been brought up mainly within the firm and coaxed, vetted and selected in accordance with the firm's principles. Started by the brothers Gerard and Anton Philips, an inventor and a businessman, in 1891, the firm is now controlled by a supervisory board headed by Chairman Frits Philips and a board of management whose president is his son-in-law, Jonkheer H.A.C. van Riemsdijk.

Philips ranks third in the *Fortune 300* directory of the three hundred largest industrials and fifty largest banks outside the U.S. with 371,000 employees on a world-wide basis. It must remain Dutch controlled. In 1920 the N.V. Gemeenschappelijk Bezit was set up to manage the interests of the shareholders. This company, which has effective control of Philips, has ten priority shares, and under the statutes these must remain in the hands of Dutch residents. According to the 1973 annual report six of the ten priority shares are held by 'Dr A.F. Philips Stichting', a foundation in the Netherlands Antilles and the remaining four are held by Frits Philips and three other members of the board of management of N.V. Gemeenschappelijk Bezit.

The use of the Gemeenschappelijk Bezit structure in order to transfer the voting power of the ordinary shareholder to a single body controlled by a smaller group of preferential shareholders is not at all uncommon in the Netherlands. In this way the family firms raise their capital on the free market and still maintain control.

The Dutch Multinationals

A different type of power is enjoyed by a company like Royal Dutch/Shell, which tops the *Fortune 300* list. Shell has relatively little contact with the rest of Dutch industry through its board of directors, although it does have contacts with the banks. Shell has such a multinational character that it does not need the Netherlands as much as the Netherlands needs Shell – a fact made painfully clear during the early stages of the Arab oil boycott at the end of 1973 when the Dutch premier Joop den Uyl was completely upstaged by Shell's senior managing director Gerrit Wagner. His sparse television appearances were followed with the same kind of reverence as General de Gaulle used to command.

The Netherlands attracts multinational companies because it is a small country with little obvious political power – despite its political pretensions – with a degree of stability which is clearly reflected in the rock-hard nature of the Dutch guilder during all the monetary fluctuations which have rocked the money market recently. The multinational companies would not come, however, if the fiscal climate were not made relatively attractive. Multinationals gravitate towards the Netherlands even when they are not founded there because holding companies are able to limit their tax liabilities by only publishing minimum accounts. DAF Houdstermaatschappij B.V., the heart of the Van Doorne motor-car concern and now listed 248th in the *Fortune 300* and linked with Volvo and IHC, publishes a profit and loss account of only seven relevant figures.

ESTEL is another example of how a Dutch company has grown into a multinational organisation. Hoogovens steelworks, which is state controlled, has now combined with the larger but weaker German Hoesch to form ESTEL, the fourth largest steel company in Europe. The ESTEL organisation is extremely complex, but it is based on a group of holding companies (see Fig. 3). In 1966 Hoesch merged with Dortmund-Horder Huttenunion A.G., in which Hoogovens had a 43 per cent share. After the Hoogovens-Hoesch merger in June 1972 this became a 14.5 per cent share in Hoesch which tipped the balance in favour of the Dutch although on paper the Dutch and Germans have equal strength on the boards of management. Chairman of the board of management is one of Holland's most approachable industrialists Poul Justman Jacob.

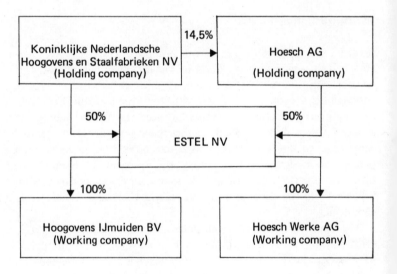

Fig. 3. The basic structure of the ESTEL organisation.

In the alliance of another key Dutch company, Fokker, with the West German Vereinigte Flugtechnische Werke from Bremen they decided on a straight 50/50 partnership with a Dusseldorf headquarters. The firm is now VFW-Fokker, and the structure is similar to that of ESTEL. It was ironic that Fokker, whose founder Anthony Fokker died embittered in New York in 1939, has now returned to the country where its founder developed fighter-bombers for the Luftwaffe while the Netherlands was trying to walk the thin line of neutrality during World War I. Nevertheless Dutch influence in the North European aircraft industry syndicate has been strengthened considerably by this merger, and the Netherlands is assured a steady share in the market for military aircraft despite the criticism by other NATO partners that the Dutch are not pulling their weight in NATO.

In shipping, a more traditional Dutch industry, mergers under pressure of foreign competition have lead to the formation of the Rijn-Schelde-Verolmeconcern, 174th in the *Fortune 300*. The merger was one of the few dramatic occurrences on the Dutch industrial scene to be played out in the full glare of publicity. It marked the end of the reign of one of Holland's most eccentric industrial figures, Cornelis Verolme, a loner who devoted a lifetime to creating a large part of the Dutch shipbuilding and repair industry. Verolme's reluctance to relinquish power and his concern for the future of his company, a heritage which he wanted to pass on to those who had helped build it, marked the end of an era.

Cornelis Verolme was born in 1900 and was forty six before he started single-handed on his shipbuilding career. He was deeply distrusted by his rivals, and by the Dutch government too, because he did not fit into the system where banks and industry and government, closely linked, kept one another in business. Cornelis Verolme, a deeply religious Calvanist, claims that his whole empire was built on the principle of ploughing back every cent of profit. He dismisses all speculation that he raised capital with loans from everyone from Onassis and the Shah of Persia to the gnomes of Zurich. Whether for business reasons or out of pure jealousy, Dutch industry within the conventional system has consistently refused to believe him. But during his reign Dutch company law could not compel Cornelis Verolme to publish facts and figures, and he was not inclined to reveal the secrets of the financing of his multi-million world-wide empire.

The Aristocracy in Industry

It has often been suggested that the Dutch Royal family has a considerable interest in Dutch industry. Prince Bernhard, the supreme industrial ambassador for the Netherlands, has said that there are at least twenty people in the Netherlands richer than his wife, Queen Juliana. The myth of the royal family's wealth was exploded when the Dutch lost Indonesia after World War II. Queen Wilhelmina had very considerable investments in the former Dutch colony and the royal fortune was seriously eroded when, after ill-calculated skirmishes, the Dutch Government finally conceded what was a long-established fact and gave Indonesia all except West Irian.

The Dutch aristocracy, however, retains its industrial rôle for a variety of reasons. Just like the British longing for a lord on the board, Dutch companies like to have a Jonkheer somewhere on the list. The Dutch aristocracy, in so far as it still exists, has to work for its living and is always glad of an extra source of income. On the other hand most of the Jonkheren on Dutch boards of supervision or management have had to prove their worth either in government, diplomacy, banking or industry before getting the chance of a seat in the boardroom.

The president of the board of management of AKZO, Holland's largest chemical concern, is Jonkheer Kraijenhoff, an example of an aristocrat who has earned his place with sheer hard work and endurance. He is also chairman of the Dutch Red Cross, and a vice-chairman of the Red Cross Liga in Geneva.

The most powerful aristocrat is probably Jonkheer Feith, in 1970 president of the supervisory boards of Van Gelder, Heineken and the Nederlandse Dagblad Unie, and member of the supervisory boards of Berkel Patent, the AMRO bank and Robeco. He is closely followed by C.T. Graaf Lynden van Sandenburg, former Queen's commissioner for the province of Utrecht and former member of the Social Economic Council, the main consultative body which advises the Government on all social economic questions, and in 1970 member of the supervisory boards of Heineken, Thomassen en Drijver Verblifa, the Steenkool Handelsvereniging (SHV, controlled by the Fentener van Vlissingen family) and the Netherlands Central Bank.

Politico-economic Elite

In the Autumn of 1971 Dr F.N. Stockman and Professor R.J. Mokken at the Department of Political Science of Amsterdam University carried out an unpublished study of the patterns of influence among the economic and political élite in the Netherlands. Even taking into account the limitations of the study, it is nevertheless interesting to note the central position of the banks. In a computer analysis of the connections between boards of directors the central position of the AMRO bank in particular emerged. It came above the larger Algemene Bank Nederland and Rabobank (50 and 42 in the *Fortune 300*) and the influential Mees en Hope Bank. Not taken into the survey were the smaller but no less important merchant-type banks such as van Lanschot, Slavenburgs, and Pierson, Heldring and Pierson, again institutions with a basic family background or structure.

Of the twenty eight leading businessmen listed in the Amsterdam survey with six or more seats on governing boards, only two did *not* have at least one post on the board of a bank or a leading insurance company. (Insurance companies, like the banks, are an important source of capital in the Netherlands). Out of the forty leading businessmen with five or more boardroom seats, only three had no seat on the board of a bank. The bank with the most business links of this kind was AMRO. It is interesting to see that, while the large, predominantly domestic Dutch firms usually have several directors with seats on the boards of related firms, the multi- and internationals remain isolated. No analysis of their directors' positions abroad has been attempted, but it would probably reveal that the directors occupy other strategic boardroom seats but at an international level. The AMRO bank, however, has two of its directors usefully placed on the boards of Shell, Unilever and Philips.

Influence at Work

Interesting as these patterns of inter-relationship may be it is yet more interesting to see what this means in practice. The fact that a contact between firms exists does not necessarily mean that it is used to the full. On the other hand Dutch directors do not collect boardroom seats merely to pocket their fee. A seat on a Dutch board is generally only for those who are willing to work, and that includes members of the majority shareholding family. The strategic position of the banks means that they have access to inside information and can quickly adapt their investment policy on the stock exchange to take advantage of it. Also access to this information means that the banks are able to take quick decisions on company demands for credit facilities and capital. The banks' influence on the company can be exercised in various ways. They sometimes demand a shareholding, but since the power of the Dutch shareholder is strictly limited in most large firms, this is little more than a form of security. The influence on company policy does not come from the floor of the annual shareholders' meeting, but in theboardroom itself. If a company is in difficulties and does not follow thebank's instructions it is swiftly bankrupted. Under this threat a change in company policy, including a thorough reorganisation, is oftencarried out so that part of the firm can be saved, and the rest sold off. The rôle of the banks, with their privileged inside information, has often been criticised. Yet it must be said in their favour that the more conservative family-owned Dutch industries often need to be forced to shake off the inertia of nepotism and to recruit outside management to save the jobs of hundreds of employees. The Amsterdam survey concluded that a close knit network of contacts between companies through common directors controls and regulates the availability of capital for Dutch industry. The number of people involved is even fewer than the 200 Mertens spoke of. The basic list of key figures is reduced to sixty names. But that list includes few of those who might rank as industrial barons in their own right. There is no Philips, Fentener van Vlissingen, Heineken, Von Thyssen-Bornemisza or even a Van Doorne.

Key Figures

It is worthwhile putting the spotlight on a few at the top of the list, even if their boardroom functions do read like a rollcall of prominent Dutch businesses. It is the only way to illustrate how the system works. Take, for instance Professor dr J.R. van der Brink, generally believed to be the most influential man in Dutch industrial circles. He is a director of the AMRO bank. At the time of the Amsterdam survey he was president of the supervisory boards of Eerste Nilmij (now Ennia), the large insurance company, of SHV, the vast mining and trading concern, and of AKZO, the major Dutch chemical concern. He also had seats on the supervisory boards of Rijn-Schelde, now merged with Verolme to consolidate almost all Dutch shipbuilding, of Gist-Brocades (chemicals, pharmaceuticals and foodstuffs) and of the Dutch Railways. He was on the board of management of Koninklijke Nederlands Paper (paper). Seen in conjunction with his position as a leading member of the Roman Catholic political party (KVP) and his past experience as Minister of Economic Affairs, one can claim he has a finger in every aspect of Dutch policy-making. Take for instance, M.W. van der Wall Bake, acting chairman of the supervisory board of the Algemene Bank Nederland, but also member of the supervisory board of the National Investment Bank, the most important financial guarantor for the launching of Dutch subsidiaries abroad and particularly in developing countries. His boardroom seats include Robeco, the largest investment company outside the U.S., V.M.F. (machine engineering), Fokker (aircraft), KNSM (shipbuilding, Delta Lloyd (now owned by Commercial Union) and Hoogovens (now ESTEL) steelworks.

Further down the list, an interesting example of government-industrial connections, is F.J. van Thiel, retired chairman of the Dutch Second Chamber – a function to be compared wth the Speaker of the House of Commons – but simultaneously a leading force in the Protestant camp with seats on the boards of Rijn-Schelde, Delta Lloyd and A.B.N. This combined with his various governmentposts made Van Thiel, now retired, a highly influential contact between government, political parties and industry. During Holland's televised parliamentary debates Van Thiel achieved the status of a nationally popular figure while confidently wielding the chairman's gavel. Few members of the public, however, were aware of the functions he carried out behind the scenes.

The Background of Power

The leading Dutch businessmen have, we can conclude, a standard and typical pattern of behaviour. But where do they come from? It is easier to define where their origins do *not* lie than to trace a common line. They are not products of public schools or any other private educational system, they do not wear the same club tie, they do not play golf or cricket and they have no time and little inclination to show the outside world that they live according to their status.

One fairly common factor in their background is the University of Leiden, which also produces much of the foreign service. The first step towards a seat on the boad is often a Leiden degree – generally in law – or in Roman Catholic circles a Tilburg or a Nymegen economics degree. Before Leiden most top businessmen have passed through the standard Dutch education system, the *gymnasium* with either a grounding in the classics or the sciences. The happy few, mostly members of prominent families, have been to secondary or finishing school in Switzerland.

But to get to the roots of the personality of the Dutch businessman it is necessary to go much further back, to the golden age of the Dutch patricians and the days of the East India Company. The Dutch Calvanist tradition has turned the people into a God-fearing nation, but one which is capable of bending its morality to breaking point when it is a question of trade. Dutch politicians and the Protestant and Roman Catholic churches have repeatedly condemned South Africa, while apparently living unaware in a society whose prosperity is partially based on the fruits of apartheid. The rise in the wages of African labour in South Africa has severely damaged the profits of several prominent Dutch international companies. Many of the Dutch still dislike the Germans, and any suggestion that the three war criminals still serving life sentences in Breda gaol should be freed triggers off a wave of emotion among those who suffered from the effects of World War II German occupation. But Rotterdam's port and insurance facilities are 80 per cent German owned; ESTEL, Fokker-VFW, Thyssen Bornemisza are all irrevocably interwoven with German industry. The Dutch guilder and the Dutch balance of payments benefit from the buoyancy of the West German economy. And today Dutch society is even learning to let married women work. The churches in Holland have traditionally disapproved of married women working on purely moral grounds. But now that industry in the Netherlands needs married women in the factories as a cheap alternative to expensive foreign imported labour, morality has changed. All of a sudden it is recognised that a married woman can best contribute to the development and stability of her family if she retains her contact with the outside world. Should the labour market change dramatically, it will be fascinating to observe the moral swing which will inevitably accompany it.

Inscrutability and Wealth

It is said that the Dutch were the first to be allowed to do business in China because they were the only ones who were willing to spit on the cross in order to gain Chinese favour. Comparisons between the Dutch and the Chinese have often been made – especially by the Dutch. The peculiar Dutch reluctance to reveal their christian names – almost a better kept secret in industrial circles than their accounts – is symptomatic. In an annual report in Holland the members of the board will cheerfully print their ages, but not their first names.

In order to maintain the system, it is essential that the best brains in Dutch society are syphoned into industry. Ex-foreign minister Norbert Schmelzer and ex-premier Barend Biesheuvel were promptly offered advisory posts with the H.B.G. and with Unilever respectively after they were voted out of office. Andre Kloos, ex-chairman of the powerful socialist trade union NVV, and now head of the socialist VARA broadcasting organisation, is now on the supervisory board of ESTEL representing the employees. His immediate successor, Harry ter Heide, who only remained in office for a short time, is now on the AMRO board.

The Netherlands is historically an agricultural society. Its people live close to the ground. In a country where more than half the area is under sea level people remain sensitive to the power of the elements. The Dutch climate and the Dutch morality have turned the Netherlands into a rudimentary jungle in Europe where only the physically and mentally fit survive. In Holland's political society there is room for the dissident. The Dutch have historically been the first to accept the outcasts of other societies; Jews, Hugenots, Catholics and other sects, and more recently Czechs, Hungarians, Greeks, Chileans – they are all welcome. So long as they can work.

This agricultural folk, anchored in its own morality, where the Calvanists stand their ground – and as a result the Catholics along the Reformation border are more Calvanist than the Calvanists – have learned to temper politics in order to preserve their right to exist. Concessions are essential, on both sides.

The leading figures in Dutch business life can only be seen through a glass darkly, because they like it that way. The closed family circle is still the best defence against foreign intruders. If Dutch businesses had a collective coat of arms, their motto would be the old saying 'Geld Stinkt Niet' – money has no stench.

CHAPTER 7 BELGIUM & LUXEMBOURG: THE POWER OF 'LES HOLDINGS'

Anthony Rowley

Remember that the King of the Netherlands always has money available for industry . . . William I to John Cockerill

The Société Générale

William of Orange it was indeed who in 1822 established the original Société Générale which was to finance the growth of a great part of Belgian industry and which today remains by far the most important single force in the country's economic life. Société Générale, or 'La Générale' as it is usually called, is a vast industrial holding company cum banking empire which controls anything between 25 and 50 per cent of Belgian manufacturing industry. No-one knows for certain just how much because of the tortuous inter-twinings of its interlocked holdings in numerous subsidiaries, which in turn have subsidiaries of their own. Grouped together, these planets and outer stars in the Société Générale universe probably account for one-third of Belgium's national income. La Générale lists the Belgian royal family as well as the Vatican among its shareholders in addition to that all-powerful family alliance behind Belgian business – the Solvays, the Boëls and the Janssens. Belgian industry and commerce is to all intents and purposes controlled by a dozen powerful holdings companies – *les holdings* – of which the second biggest after La Générale (though still a good deal smaller) is the Compagnie Lambert pour l'Industrie et la Finance, domain of the Baron Lambert whose business fortunes are now linked with those of another famous Belgian family, the De Launoits. Belgium's is a unique tradition of capitalism which defies direct comparison probably anywhere in the world.

How Société Générale came so to dominate Belgium's industrial and financial life is a story rooted in the country's recent economic history. When Belgium was stripped away from France and forcibly unified with Holland after the fall of Napoleon, a basically industrial or artisan state, Belgium, was allied with a country of commerce, Holland. Société Générale was intended to become a microcosm of this economically complementary union. Belgium was at that time famous for its handwoven wool and linen, for its brassware, for the gunsmiths of Liège and for craftsmen of every kind, but it did not have capital on anything like the scale needed to finance the dawning age of mechanised industry. William I, who had received an English upbringing and had seen the Industrial Revolution there, set up what was originally called the 'Société Générale des Pays-Bas pour favoriser l'Industrie Nationale' to supply this much needed capital. Until then industrial credit simply did not exist in Belgium.

Fortunes at that time consisted mainly of real estate and few were prepared to venture their capital in industry. La Générale was at the outset, a land bank, a savings bank and a house with the privilege of issuing bank notes. But its original memorandum of incorporation provided that it should also supply development funds for industry, by way of loans or in some cases by shareholdings. Unfortunately the initial offer of shares for general subscription in La Générale was no great success and King William effectively underwrote the issue by taking up the majority of the shares himself. La Générale grew in importance and was also invested with the office of State Cashier and the Bank of Issue for the Belgian part of the Kingdom of the Netherlands. It was supposed to be the channel for the flow of business between Belgian industry and Dutch commerce but was 'largely unmindful of its industrial functions in the early years'.

The Kingdom of the Netherlands was to prove short-lived and after Belgium declared its independence in 1830 La Générale offered its funds to the new Provisional Government. It was a long time before William forgave this 'act of treachery to its former prince' though eventually he recognised Belgium and the integrity of Société Générale as part of an independent Belgium. He was later bought out of his shareholding in the Société Générale. La Générale had lost its tithe rights in Holland but it maintained forest land in Belgium after independence and these were progressively sold off to provide funds for the country's industrialisation. Through the issue of further capital and the expansion of its loan capital, Société Générale grew into a kind of universal bank on the German model and in the 1830s helped finance the country's railway system. It also assisted in the financing of collieries, blast furnaces, canals and refineries largely through the offices of the then Governor of Société Générale, Ferdinand, Count de Meeûs. La Générale spawned subsidiaries which were banks on the German lines. These were prepared to take shares in the industrial enterprises rather than avoiding long-term industrial credit or shareholdings as the British clearing banks did. It was thus by promptly subscribing shares in the capital of industrial companies and by making long-term investments that La Générale acquired many of its present day holdings in industry and service trades. Apart from this development of marrying banking with industry ownership, the Société Générale had another innovation to its credit, the formation of what was in effect the first investment trust, the 'Société des Capitalistes Réunis dans un But de Mutualité Industrielle' in 1837. Its job was to place funds in a large number of firms as an insurance 'against the temporary reverses any one of these may suffer'.

In 1838 the rival Banque de Belgique succumbed to the general crisis in Europe and closed its doors but the Société Générale, supported by the Rothschilds, remained open, paying out coin against the notes issued by its competitor. The financial crisis deepened through the following ten years and La Générale had to ask for the Government's help. A National Bank was formed and the Société ceased to be state cashier and issuer of note. It had lost its official character, liquidated its landed property and now turned entirely to providing commercial credit and acting as an industrial development company. La Générale recovered quickly from its earlier misfortunes and soon its reserves were as big as its capital. It then decided on another innovation – the 'capitalising' of these reserves and the issuing of equity shares or *parts de réserve* against them. The original capital shares continued to carry fixed interest but the new shares were entitled to dividends. This was later to form the pattern of the British system of preference and ordinary shares. But there were two reasons why industry ownership in Belgium evolved its own peculiar pattern. First, it was to a vast umbrella organisation or holding company that investors were subscribing capital, rather than to individual enterprises and secondly, the system of anonymous 'bearer' shares in Belgium rather than that of shares registered in the name of the holder meant that the influence of the small shareholder in the running of the business was much less.

The method of financing the Belgian railway system is a useful example of how the Société Générale worked. Several years are needed for the laying of a line and in that time the railway company of course has no revenues and can offer only bonds or shares to pay for the equipment they need. Such payment was of no use to the metal manufacturing companies, who themselves needed working capital. So, the usual pattern was for La Générale to set up a formal railway holding company and to place its bonds and shares among the public in return for a cash subscription, in order to finance the work. A similar method of financing was evolved for the coal and iron industries. In Britain or the U.S.A. the pattern would probably have been for the individual enterprises to go direct to the public (via the Stock Exchange) to place their bonds and shares but in Belgium the intervention of an intermediary – La Générale – helped give it the powerful hold it still exercises over many of the country's basic industries. In fact many English firms had been given the job of railway construction in Belgium but 'were more interested in stock jobbing profits than in the coherent linking up of the lines'.[14] So in order to unify the whole railway network, the Belgian Government bought it up in 1876 with (inevitably) the Société Générale subscribing to the 240 million Belgian franc loan for this purpose.

From coal, steel and transport, La Générale extended its interests to railway systems abroad and in 1898 took a large shareholding in Compagnie Électrique Anversoise, which later subscribed a quarter of the capital of Société d'Électricité de l'Escaut. The two were later integrated to become the EBES (Sociétés Réunies d'Energie du Bassin de l'Escaut) of today, which is Belgium's biggest producer and distributor of electric power and which also markets gas and steam. It was Société Générale also that financed the tramways (which incidentally Belgium pioneered throughout the world) through its subsidiary, Compagnie Mutuelle des Tramways, now known as Traction et Électricité. In metallurgy too, La Générale subsidiaries, including Cockerill were spreading Belgian technology throughout and beyond Europe. In shipping Belgium's connections with the Congo were spurring progress on and, here again, La Générale was prominent, providing short- and long-term credits. In 1906 under Leopold II Belgium was moving toward the height of its colonial adventure in the Congo and three companies were formed under the auspices of Société Générale to extract copper in Katanga and to transport it by rail to the coasts for shipment to Europe. The three were Union Minière, Forminière and Chemin de Fer du Bas-Congo au Katanga. Of this trio, Union Minière survives to this day as one of La Générale's most successful subsidiaries, prospecting for minerals in Canada and Australia, now that the Congo interests are far less significant. From the Congo — where it was said to have controlled 90 per cent of Belgium's interests in the country's colonial heyday — La Générale moved much farther afield and extended its operations to imperial China for the financing of railways and other services.

In the Great War of 1914–18 it was the Société Générale that again took over the issue of banknotes and after the war set about making funds available for the country's economic restoration. La Générale was at this time investing widely — in energy, non-ferrous metals, iron and steel, mechanical and electrical engineering, in chemicals, in ocean transport, in textiles and in glass. It was acquiring shareholdings, setting up new companies, and extending its interests, not only in Belgium but also in Luxembourg and the Congo. It also formed a big textile co-operative known as La Textile. La Générale also bought into Ateliers de Constructions Électriques de Charleroi (ACEC) in 1920. ACEC is the Brussels-based electrical engineering combine in which Westinghouse of the U.S.A. has since taken a 68 per cent interest. La Générale also bought into the chemical and glass industries around 1920 as well as helping to form Petrofina the petroleum and oil group, in which it still has a direct stake. In 1927 La Générale took up shares in what is now Belgium's biggest steel company, Cockerill and the following year acquired a large number of shares in ARBED (Aciéries Réunis de Burbach-Eich-Dudelange) which today is by far the largest company in the Grand Duchy of Luxembourg. The Société's activities around this time also included co-operating with the Government in the re-organisation of Lloyd Royal Belge the shipping line and it was linked with the formation of SABENA, the national Belgian airline.

In 1934, after the great slump and the accompanying run on the banks, came the passing of an Act in Belgium which changed the face of banking, separating deposit banking from investment banking and which changed the very name of La Générale. The original name had meant 'company for the promotion of the Nation's Industry'. Now two companies were formed — the Société Générale de Banque, consolidating virtually all of La Générale's old banking interests, and Société Générale de Belgique, consolidating all the industrial interests. This latter is what most people mean nowadays when they refer to 'La Générale'. Much later, in 1960, this division was emphasised when it was decided in consultation with the national Commission Bancaire that no chairman of SG de Banque should also sit on the board of SG de Belgique. The legal partitioning of the former 'mixed' banks was thereby solidified.

During the 1939—45 war the Société Générale became a principal instrument for protecting the interests of the Belgians against the occupying German Nazi régime and it supported the Resistance movement (necessarily) covertly through organising the sale of goods on the black market to give financial aid to the movement. After the war, the changed pattern of economic life was reflected in the portfolio of Société Générale. Its interests in collieries had declined but those in electricity (including nuclear power) and oil as well as in finance and specialised engineering had grown. The African interests have diminished while new ones, in Canada and elsewhere (Union Minière etc.) have grown. As La Générale grew bigger, management problems grew proportionately and the present 'Governor', M. Max Nokin, followed the lead set by his predecessor, M. Paul Gillet, in consolidating activities around 'pivot' firms in each sector and selling off peripheral interests. The new image of La Générale is summed up in the construction of its present-day portfolio. Nearly 90 per cent of its investment interests are in five sectors and a third of these in finance and banking (Société Générale de Belgique being the biggest shareholder in its sister organisation Société Générale de Banque, which is now the biggest bank in Belgium) while more than a quarter are in non-ferrous metals and diamonds. A tenth of the interests are in steel and a similar proportion in energy and engineering. Contracting and construction activities account for a further 8 per cent. There are also interests in shipping, transport, chemicals, glass, textiles and paper.

The principal 'pivot' companies are Société Générale de Banque, specialising in all forms of deposit and commercial banking; Sofina the chief financing subsidiary, also specialising in investment banking; Sibéka (Société d'Entreprises et d'Investissements) in non-ferrous metals and other minerals; Traction et Électricité in energy and civil engineering; Arbed the Luxembourg steel group; Union Minière; Metallurgie Hoboken-Overpelt the non-ferrous metal group; CBR the cement company; the Companhia de Diamantes de Angola (self-explanatory) and, last but by no means least, Cockerill, the Belgian iron and steel giant. There are many more subsidiaries (a full list is appended) though the precise shareholding in each is not possible to determine because, as mentioned above, of the interlocking holdings of one subsidiary in another. La Générale does not believe in producing consolidated sets of profit figures as a diversified British or American group would. As the finance director, M. René Lamy, says: 'It would be misleading to add up a quarter of this, an eighth of that and two per cent of another and to say that these added-up bits of companies's sales are our turnover.'

La Générale has equally definite views against presenting a technological image simply for the purposes of appearing 'modern' and more glamorous. When the Brussels daily newspaper, *La Libre Belgique*, asked M. Nokin recently why Société Générale was not better represented in advanced industrial sectors, he replied:

'We will always continue to use cement, but we are not sure that tomorrow we will still use as much of such and such a product which is in the limelight at the moment. The terrific technical evolution makes advanced industries very vulnerable and we don't have the right to centre the greater part of our activities on fragile sectors.'

This attitude is reflected in the fact that La Générale is strong still in those industries whose roots go back to the nineteenth century – coal, steel and transport for instance – but weak in aerospace and electronics. But if expansion is not going to be strong in areas of advanced technology (in the short term at least) there is every intention of becoming more international.

The Catholic review *La Revue Nouvelle* once compared Société Générale with the American colussus ITT (on which, see Anthony Sampson).[15] ITT, said the author, was like a modern building, functional and produced at one go, whereas La Générale was like 'an old château, patched and ill-assorted, where different styles and epochs are superimposed and co-exist come what may.' But the 'château' has already seen some of its more rambling wings demolished. A few years ago the Société Générale had around 100 companies in its portfolio. Now it has seventy-two and the figure will perhaps fall to around twenty eventually.[16] As this number falls the intention is that the degree of control over those remaining will rise. As the holding company concentrates, so the affiliates diversify. Union Minière for instance, after making its fortune mining copper in the Congo, saw its assets there nationalised in 1967 and has since invested in data processing, aerospace and nuclear power as well as concentrating in mining in Canada and Australia. Sofina, the financial subsidiary (which in many ways resembles Compagnie Lambert, see below) is run by M. Jean Rey, former head of the European Commission. La Générale, itself cautious towards new risk-capital ventures, uses Sofina as a monkey's paw to test new areas of investment, such as oil, food and home furnishings. Another highly diversified affiliate is Genstar (appropriately named as it is one of SG's star performers) which is the successor to Sogemines the Canadian mining company La Générale set up in the 1950's. Genstar is itself a holding company and has invested in shipping, real estate and public works and construction.

Unlike other Belgian holding companies, La Général takes a direct part in the management of its affiliates instead of simply investing money in them. Thus the deputy Governor, M. Paul-Emile Corbiau is also chairman and managing director of Metallurgie Hoboken-Overpelt, while M. Nokin himself holds a similar position in the cement company, Cimenteries CBR. Through the passivity of other shareholders in those companies where it has stakes and because of its interlocking holdings, La Générale has an influence which belies the size of its holding on paper. It has a stake of only 2.2 per cent for instance in Sidmar, the modern steel firm near Ghent but through affiliates like Arbed,

Group
Société Générale

Main Interests	% of assets		10 largest holdings (BFr. m) capital	profit
Banking		17·4		
Société Génerale de Banque (20·4) (Deposits BFr. 186,909m profits BFr. 952m)	14·0		9,332	952
Banque Belge pour l'Etranger (25)				
Banque Belge Ltd				
Holding Companies		13·1		
Sofina (25)	7·7		5,448	644
Financière du Katanga (7·6)				
Congo pour le Commerce† (CCCI) (21·5)				
Union Financière et Industrielle Liégeoise (62·5)				
Non-ferrous metals and minerals		29·7		
Sibéka (52·5)	10·7		3,024	330
Metallurgie Hoboken-Overpelt (15·3 directly, plus 43·7 indirectly)	6·6		5,250	651*
Union Minière (5·9 plus 11·9 indirectly)	6·1		13,248	1,468
Companhia de Diamantes de Angola (11·5 plus 5·9 indirectly)	4·0		1,857	546
Steel		12·9		
Cockerill (12·9)	4·3		15,320	1,107
Arbed (14·8)	7·0		20,735	1,648
Sidmar (2·3 plus 29 indirectly)				
Electricity				
Traction et Electricité (23·2 plus 19·2 indirectly)	6·3		2,435	226
Real estate and construction		6·7		
Cimenteries CBR (23·8)	3·3		2,476	189
Mechanical & electrical		4·7		
ACEC (6·4)				
Brugeoise et Nivelles				
Other		9·7		
		100.0	79,125	7,761

Control
Autonomous. Large shareholders believed to be Belgian Royal Family, the Vatican, Prince Amaury de Merode, Count Lippens, Solvay/Boël/Janssen families.

Value
Net book value BFr. 6,457m (since increased to BFr. 8,570m) Net market value BFr. 20,909m (counting deposits from affiliates) Net profit BFr. 714m

*Figures in brackets show percentage owned *15 months †now Eurotremer*
1970 figures

Fig. 4. The present-day structure of La Sociéte Générale de Belgique group

Cockerill and Union Minière it in fact controls nearly 63 per cent of the equity. Members of the Société Générale family account for about 15 per cent of the manpower in Belgian manufacturing industry, 40 per cent of all deposits in private commercial banks, 90 per cent of national non-ferrous metals output, 67 per cent of steel output and 50 per cent of cement output. Group companies are also the largest in Belgium in insurance, construction and public works, engineering, textiles, paper, industrial diamonds and diamond tools. They are also prominent in public utilities, mechanical and electrical manufacture and fertilisers. (See full list appended.)

Though as a holding company Société Générale de Belgique employs few more than 200 people, the payroll of its affiliates and subsidiaries is 260,000 of whom some 200,000 work in Belgium. There are many ways of valuing La Générale. Its own estimate[17] (as of 31 December 1972) is that capital and reserves attributable to shareholders are B. Frs 9,167,869,486 (9.2 billion) but its shareholding portfolio, shown in the balance sheet at B. Frs 9 billion had an actual stock market value at that time nearer B. Frs 22 billion. Operating profits in 1972 were around B. Frs 1,000 million.

La Générale likes to point out that it has 'tens of thousands' of shareholders though its true ownership remains an enigma because so few of these shares are registered in the names of the holders, the remainder being anonymous bearer shares tucked away in banks. However, the Belgian royal family and the Solvay family are the only major shareholders apart from, of course, the cross holdings within the group, according to an SG spokesman. Only about 250 shareholders ever turn up at annual general meetings to rubber stamp the board's decisions and so the directors and top management tend to be a 'self-perpetuating oligarchy'.[18] Ironically, La Générale is itself currently trying to find out more about the identity of its smaller shareholders. Holders of the bearer shares show no enthusiasm for selling them for capital gain (despite the lack of a capital gains tax in Belgium) and the group is thus enable to get its stock market value up. This is a hindrance when it comes to having rights issues to existing shareholders to raise cash, as the stock market price then determines the new issue price. Société Générale is a remarkable institution. Perhaps the best description of it was that given by M. Eugene-G. de Barsy, president of the Commission Bancaire in his message sent to the governor, M. Nokin during the 150th anniversary celebrations. 'Economic history,' wrote M. de Barsy, 'has made of the group a reality of an unusual type, unique, scarcely yielding to definition yet so real, so vital, so important and in spirit so national.'

So much for eulogy: not all Belgians see the holding companies in an equally favourable light. Some indeed see them as sprawling octopuses exercising a stranglehold over Belgium's economy; autocratic, sometimes arrogant, stifling innovation and suppressing the rights of small shareholders. M. Henri Simonet, now EEC Commissioner for industrial affairs and formerly Belgian Minister of Economic Affairs, took a none-too-sanguine view when he was a socialist deputy. In 1971 he introduced a Bill calling for much tougher control over the holding companies by the Commission Bancaire, regulating agency for the financial institutions. He accused the holding companies of 'laying down the law in vast industrial, commercial and financial complexes' without taking account of the wider needs of the economy or of shareholders' interests. The Bill failed and the grip of the holding companies remains as tight as ever.

Compagnie Bruxelles Lambert

The Baron Leon Lambert, chairman of Compagnie Bruxelles Lambert, Belgium's second largest holding company (though much smaller still than La Générale) takes what might be seen as a more democratic view of industry ownership. He talks of the City of London becoming the financial centre of Europe, now that Britain has joined the EEC, and of this leading to the wider ownership of shares and more active stock markets in Europe. However, some observers of the Belgium economic scene have commented, perhaps rather cynically, that this is no more than the Baron Lambert's pique at not being able to wrest more control of industry from the omnipotent and ubiquitous Société Générale. In fact one of the most controversial of Belgium's few takeover bids in the past fifteen years involved Compagnie Lambert and its move for control of Sofina, the holding company in which La Générale has a 25 per cent interest. Lambert had been a frustrated minority shareholder in Sofina for many years. However, the powerful Boël family, together with the French bank, Lazard Frères were also shareholders. They decided to fight the Lambert bid and, closing ranks with La Générale itself and with Mediobanca from Italy, another shareholder, they successfully fought it off. 'Ever since this alarming breach of traditional calm, the links between the Générale and the Boëls and their relatives by marriage, the Solvays and the Janssen families, have been strengthening.'[19] This was not the only case of strife between the barons of

Belgian industry. ACEC, the electrical group mentioned above, was controlled jointly by the Société Générale and by Baron Empain, the rich young financier-industrialist after the war. Neither would cede control to the other, however, to the detriment of ACEC and eventually more than two-thirds of its shares passed into American hands — the hands of Westinghouse to be precise. In the late 1960s Westinghouse almost succeeded in gaining control of another of the Baron Empain's interests, Jeumont-Schneider, the electro-mechanical engineering group in France but the French Government stepped in and demanded a 'French solution', politely showing Westinghouse the door in the process.

But to return to Compagnie Lambert. Its origins go back to 1840 when Samuel Lambert opened an agency in Antwerp for the Rothschilds of Paris. Samuel was Leon's great grandfather, his grandfather having married a Rothschild and his father having become an independent banker. It was Leon's father who guaranteed the autonomy of the Banque Lambert *vis-à-vis* Paris, though Rothschilds have continued to sit on the bank's board and have a small stake in the equity. Baron Leon took over the family company in 1949 when it was a small deposit bank and in 1953 formed Compagnie Lambert, the holding company, merging that with the bank itself in 1959. It concentrated largely on financial services and the Baron has built up the reputation of something of a financial whizz kid, in Belgian terms at least.

His grand coup came toward the end of 1972 when he brought off, against a great deal of opposition and almost machiaevelian manoeuvrings, a merger of Compagnie Lambert pour la Finance et l'Industrie with three other holding companies, Brufina, Confindus and Cofinter to form the Compagnie Bruxelles Lambert. The new group's gross assets are worth nearly B. Frs 15,000 million and are deployed in banking and insurance (22 per cent), real estate (17 per cent), breweries, food and distribution (12 per cent), oil (10 per cent), public utilities (9 per cent) and steel and metal goods (8 per cent). This makes the new Lambert group much bigger than it was but La Générale still exceeds it in size, not least through the fact that its assets are some B. Frs 7 billion greater than Lambert's. Compagnie Lambert set about the merger virtually by stealth. Not that it is ever easy to know what is going on beneath the placid surface anyway, given that shares are in anonymous bearer form and transactions do not have to be declared as they do in Britain or U.S.A. over a certain level (10 per cent at the time of writing). At the end of 1971, Lambert took a majority (51 per cent) stake in Cofinter by assigning in return to Cofinter a 25 per cent stake in Banque Lambert. The rest is a tortuous but a fascinating example of how tanlged is the web of Belgian industry ownership. Lambert had a 15.6 per cent stake in Brufina (Société de Bruxelles pour la Finance et l'Industrie) and just over 1 per cent of Confindus (Compagnie Financière et Industrielle) – both (inevitably) holding companies themselves. Just to complicate matters, Confindus itself had a 15.6 per cent stake in Brufina. However, the really big shareholders in 'Con' and 'Bru' were the de Launoit family, whose origins go back to 1871 when Belgian financiers and German bankers set up the Banque de Bruxelles as an investment bank. After the 1934 separation law, the bank was hived off and the rest put into Brufina. In 1937 Confindus, which was the holding company of the de Launoits, gained control of Brufina. Before the big merger with Lambert, Brufina had been selling off banking interests and strengthening its hold on steel, coal and glass. Moreover, Baron Lambert had already been working closely with the Comte Paul de Launoit and his brother, Arsene de Launoit. They probably all favoured a merger by that stage though some of the shareholders in Banque de Bruxelles (a de Launoit interest remember) such as Barclays Bank were equally probably against Lambert gaining control of the bank and merging it with his own banking interests.

The really big spanner was thrown into the works however, by the French financial group, Paribas. It had a controlling interest in yet another Belgian holding company Cobepa. Cobepa in turn had a stake in Confindus and Confindus was the key to the whole merger because of its own stake in Brufina. But just as Cobepa was expected to launch a counter bid for Confindus, the Belgian Government stepped in – (the Prime Minister personally intervening) – and indicated that it would not tolerate a merger which resulted in a French company having ultimate control of at least one Belgian holding company. So, the all-Belgian four-way merger went ahead finally at the end of 1972, though the Paribas interests came out of the whole affair having acquired some important steel interests from the new grouping. What was the rôle of the Société Générale in all this? No-one outside the charmed circle really knows but there were many who suspected it was in there somewhere manoeuvring to thwart Lambert's bid for increased size. Ironically, the de Launoit family has links with Société Générale as well as with Lambert. Through the merger, the Lambert group now has an even more powerful portfolio of industrial as well as financial and public utility holdings. In oil it has a stake in Petrofina and in steel in Cockerill as well as in Thy Marcinelle and in H.F. de la Chiers. In public utilities it has interests in EBES, biggest of the electric power producers, as well as in Intercom (Société Intercommunale Belge de Gaz et de l'Électricité), the second biggest electricity group. There are stakes also in Électrogaz, as well as in Électrobel (Compagnie Générale d'Entreprises Électriques et Industrielle Société Anonynme) the gas, electricity, transport and civil engineering super-utility, whose chairman is Yves Boël, as well as in Interbrabant (Union Intercommunale des Centrales Électriques du Brabant) the electricity producer, whose chairman is Baron Empain.

Baron Lambert is an urbane Oxford graduate who speaks impeccable English and whose office nowadays is a strikingly modern building in the centre of Brussels on the site of the old family house. He has said that he would welcome any steps to increase the importance of equity shares in the financing of Belgian industry. But he doubts whether this is a likely development in the short-term and feels industry would continue to rely on loans. This highlights one fascinating aspect of the Belgian holding companies. This is that the parent — 'mother' as she has been termed in the case of La Générale — collects surplus funds from all its affiliates and redistributes them according to where the need is greatest at any one time. Only as a last resort is a further issue of shares made. In some cases, companies receive interest subsidies from the Government, which guarantees repayment of the loan. Baron Lambert regards it as up to the large financial institutions (insurance companies, pension funds and the like) to lead the movement towards greater outside control of industry, but as in Belgium these tend either not to exist, or to be controlled by the holding companies anyway, this looks to be little more than a pious hope.

The Grand Family Alliance

Solvays are the descendants of two brothers (see Fig. 5). They founded the Solvay company in 1863 and it is now among the dozen largest independent chemical businesses in Europe and is particularly well known for soda and salts. One of the brothers, Ernest Solvay, discovered the basic process which was named after him, (that of making sodium carbonate from common salt and limestone). Solvay went public in 1967 but the Solvay and Boël families retain control of it through a private holding company, Union Financière Boël. The Solvay company in turn controls, directly or indirectly, more than thirty factories in twelve countries producing chemicals and plastics. In

1970, Solvay and the British chemicals group, Laporte Industries, entered into a transnational industrial and financial deal which involved pooling their peroxygen interests into a new company, Interox. The deal is one of the examples of limited industrial co-operation across national frontiers in Europe that seems to have worked well, a good deal better in fact than the more ambitious unions of the Dunlop-Pirelli type, because it had limited objectives discernible at the outset rather than a nebulous idealism. A much more far reaching deal – a bid by Britain's ICI – was rumoured in 1972 though nothing has come of it yet.

Janssens are one of the premier industrial baronies in Belgium and in fact the president of the main Janssen family company is le Baron Charles-Emmanuel.[20] He is president of UCB, Union Chemique Belge, one of Belgium's leading chemical concerns which has links with the British group Fisons, on the pharmaceuticals marketing side. In 1973 UCB also took over the U.K. manufacturers of cellulosic and plastic films, British Sidac. The Janssen family is a prolific one and is heavily represented on the board of UCB as well as on the boards of the group's other industrial interests such as Glaverbel the glassmaker. In textiles, which is Belgium's second basic industry (after metallurgy) the Janssens acquired a dominating position in 1961 when UCB took over 'Fabelta'. This company, through a series of takeovers had itself become the only major Belgian company in the field of synthetic fibres. Janssens merged the Société Belge de Banque group with the Société Générale de Banque in 1966 and that is how they became important shareholders in La Générale.

The original base of the Boël industrial empire is the Fabrique de Fer de Charleroi steelworks, but they are also important shareholders in La Générale (S.G. de Banque, that is) Traction et Électricité, Électrobel, Sofina, Solvay & Compagnie and Glaverbel. The neatly interlocking holdings of the Böel and Janssen families can be found in a host of Belgian companies and their outlook is generally in sympathy with that of Société Générale where, of course, the Solvay holding compounds the power of the trio. Inevitably there is a Baron among the Boëls, Jean Fritz Amédée as well as a Count – le Comte Réné. The board of directors of Solvay & Cie is a perfect microcosm of the wider pattern of Belgian industry ownership. Jacques Solvay is chairman of the board and there sure enough in the list of his fellow directors[21] is a Janssen (Roger) and a Boël (Yves) as well as P. Casimir-Lambert.

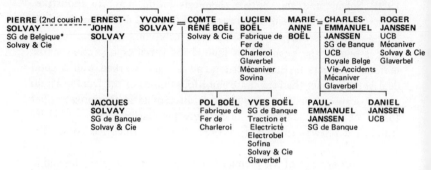

*on auditors' committee

Source: the Economist, March 18, 1972

Fig. 5. The Boel/Solvay/Janssen directorship tree.

The Solvays are the descendants of the two brothers who founded the Solvay company in 1863, now the 13th largest independent chemical business in Europe. It went public in 1967, but Solvay/Boel families keep control with a private holding company, Union Financiere Boel. Home base for the Janssens is another chemical company, UCB and Glaverbel (glass). They merged the Societe Belge de Banque group with the Societe Generale de Banque in 1966, making them important shareholders of it. The original Boel base is the Fabrique de Fer de Charleroi steelworks.

More Power Figures

There is another still powerful name in the context of Belgian industry, even if it does not have quite the ring of the names Solvay, Janssen and Boël. It is that of the Baron Edouard Jean Empain, a sort of expatriate Belgian whose business headquarters are nowadays in Paris. With the aid of a couple of dozen trusted executives, mostly Belgians, he controls from there a series of interlocking companies of 'incredible and impenetrable complexity'.[22] His holdings are mainly in France — firms such as Schneider and Creusot, formerly armaments makers, which led to Baron Empain being dubbed the 'French Krupp' — though he is in fact a Belgian national even if born 'by chance' in Hungary. The main base for his operations is 'Electrorail' a Belgian industrial holding company with extensive interests in engineering, utilities, banking and investment in Belgium and abroad, mainly in France and with its head office in the Avenue de l'Astronomie in Brussels. The 36-year-old Baron Edouard Jean — he married an Italian countess — earned the reputation of the 'sporting baron' devoting himself for a long time to his estates north of Paris, to water-skiing and to driving fast Lamborghini cars. However, the Jeumont-Schneider affair in the late 1960s meant he had to take firm control of the industrial/financial conglomerate which turns over some $800 million a year and employs 150,000 people in some 200 companies. The Baron, it is said, suffers in France from being Belgian and this indeed may have influenced General de Gaulle in his veto of a $40 million deal Baron Empain had cooked up with the American company Westinghouse. Westinghouse was all set to buy the Baron's 61 per cent holding in Jeumont-Schneider, the French heavy electrical company which makes 40 per cent of France's turbo-alternators for power stations. The Baron also has 50 per cent of Creusot-Loire, the heavy engineering group and together these holdings made him a key figure in the future of the French nuclear power industry. After de Gaulle's veto it took four years to work out a compromise whereby the French Compagnie Générale d'Électricité and Compagnie Électro-Mechanique, French subsidiary of the Swiss firm, Brown Boveri, were to carve up Jeumont-Schneider between them. Westinghouse was to be allowed to form a joint holding company with the Baron's Creusot-Loire company so that it could have a slice of the nuclear power action in France. Westinghouse took around that time a two-thirds interest in ACEC, another major Belgian electrical and engineering group, mentioned above. This was part of a concerted plan by Westinghouse to secure acceptance of its nuclear power station systems throughout western Europe, which has been at least partly successful.

If La Générale and Lambert among the holding companies together with Boëls, Solvays and Janssens among the families dominate Belgian industry ownership there are still others who cannot be ignored. There is for example the Compagnie d'Anvers a holding company whose major interests include a near 10 per cent share in Petrofina. The name of Compagnie d'Anvers also appears as a shareholder in a number of companies where La Générale has a stake, such as Traction et Électricité. True to the almost incestuous pattern of Belgian cross-holdings, the Société Générale also holds shares of the Compagnie d'Anvers itself, as does the Banque de Paris et des Pays-Bas and the Imperial Continental Gas Association. This latter group, as its name suggests, is British though it has very strong historical links with Belgium. Apart from a stake in Petrofina and the Compagnie d'Anvers it holds no less than 72 per cent of the shares of Electrogaz, the gas and electricity utility, and a smaller stake (8.5 per cent) in another electricity utility, Interbrabant.

There is le groupe Coppée, founded 120 years ago by Evence Coppée and which after the war took over management of the coalmining interests within Brufina – now part of the Lambert group. Baron Coppée is president of the group whose principal interests nowadays include La Compagnie de Développement Industriel whose business is metallurgy and chemicals and the Société de Participations Industrielles de Winterslag, a metallurgy group in which Schneider interests also have a holding. The name Coppée is also known in food production, banking and utilities.

There is also the groupe Hallet whose interests are largely in plantations though there are general financial and industrial interests also. La Bufa (l'Union Financière d'Anvers) is a holding company with interests in oil, chemicals, cement, paper and textiles while le groupe Cominière (la Société Commerciale et Minière du Congo now controlled by London based Lonrho Group) has in fact pulled back from the Congo to spread its activities in Europe. Chief among the remaining holding companies, some synonomous with ruling families, are: Nagelmackers, groupe Desclee, groupe Keglinger, groupe Plouvier, groupe Bekaert and groupe Wielemans.[23]

One of the best known of Belgian companies is la Tobacofina or just simply 'Tobacofina' as it is usually known. This is the domain of the van Zuylen and Vander Elst families, though Rothmans now has a 60 per cent interest. With financial aid from the banks (Société Générale in the main) Tobacofina has grown to dominate the Belgian tobacco industry and also manufactures in Switzerland, Africa, Indonesia and Brasil. British American Tobacco (BAT's) has a 57 per cent stake in another leading Belgian Tobacco group, Odon Warland.

Who are the Subsidiaries?

Enough has been said about the holding companies and the powerful barons behind them to show just how near absolute is their grip on Belgium's industrial life and indeed upon its economic life as Belgium proverbially 'lives by its industry'. But what of the biggest companies held by the leviathans?

Petrofina, (known to many for its FINA petrol stations) is probably Belgium's biggest company and is one of the few rising stars on the Brussels Bourse. Being as realistic as cynical, one can say that the main reasons why the company has troubled to court the shareholder in recent times (beyond, that is, La Générale and Lambert, who both have interests) is because of the prodigious sums of money required for oil exploration. In 1970, the consortium in which Petrofina has a 30 per cent stake discovered an important oil deposit in the North Sea, off Norway. Shareholders, instead of being haughtily dismissed after the usual Belgian fashion as people whose sole function is to 'clip bits of paper for dividends', have been actively courted by regular rises in dividend payments and they have seen the value of their investment rise almost astronomically of late as North Sea excitement mounted, particularly after the Arab oil cutbacks in the autumn of 1973. Petrofina is regarded as 'La Vedette' of the Brussels Bourse[24] and indeed represents a very substantial part of the total market value (capitalisation) of all shares quoted there, along with the two all-important utility companies, EBES and Intercom. Petrofina has no crude oil of its own in the Middle East or North Africa but concentrates instead on politically stable areas of exploration like the North Sea and Canada.

Petrofina's popularity with investors is however, very much an isolated phenomenon on the Brussels Bourse, which has been called the 'Cinderella' of the Belgian economy. The vast colonnaded edifice in the centre of the City is a 'sad, neglected institution'. The low level of activity on the Belgian stock market is symptomatic of the insignificant rôle it plays in the country's financial life. It reflects the almost complete lack of control the small shareholder has in the running of the industrial machine. Belgians hold bearer shares which helps tax avoidance – 'a national sport in Belgium, rivalled only by a fanatical interest in cycle racing'.[25] Most bearer shares rarely change hands and are often handed down from father to son. They only have to be registered when a shareholder wants to vote at a company meeting, and that happens very rarely. This is why the holding companies can exert almost absolute control even when they own only a small proportion of the shares, simply by registering part or all of their holdings and using them to vote. As a result, shareholders meetings are rarely anything more than 'rubber stamps' for approving decisions taken by the directors, whose number often includes members of the holding company boards anyway. Meetings are always sparsely attended and votes are taken unanimously or, if there is a dissenting voice, unanimously minus one or two.

Petrofina is to the oil industry in Belgium what Solvay is to chemicals and petrochemicals and what a company like Cockerill (Cockerill-Ougrée-Providence et Esperance-Longdoz, now merged with the former Forges de la Providence) is to steel. Cockerill is in fact the country's biggest steel company and La Générale is the biggest single share holder with just under 13 per cent of the equity. In 1971 it accounted for just under 39 per cent of national steel production. La Générale has concentrated on building the company up in recent years to match the other steel giants of the EEC, notably the British Steel Corporation, the projected Thyssen-Rheinstahl group in Germany, and Finsider in Italy.

It has cost them a good deal of money and trouble but M. Nokin, the Société Générale Governor says he believes in steel. 'It is a product which will develop in the twenty-first century.' This is typical of La Générale's concentration on basic industries, and this is a national priority too. What is good for La Générale is good for Belgium and vice versa. Metallurgie Hoboken-Overpelt (which has a small stake in Britain's Rio Tinto-Zinc Corporation) is the principal non-ferrous and precious metals group in Belgium. La Générale has a big stake (nearly 60 per cent directly or indirectly) and M. Nokin himself is on the board of directors.

State Control

In all the EEC countries, there is a smaller public sector than in Britain but in the Economic Union of Belgium and Luxembourge (BLEU) it is even smaller than elsewhere in the EEC.[26] The Belgian Government has a big share in banking and communications. It is the main shareholder in the principal Belgian airline (SABENA) – the Société Anonyme Belge d'Exploitation de la Navigation Aeriénne – and in the national railway company (SNCB) – the Société Nationale des Chemins de Fer Belges. Linked with the railways there is a network of intertown bus and tram services run by SNCV – the Société Nationale des Chemins de Fer Vicinaux. Private companies operated most of the urban tramway systems until recently but increasingly they are being taken over by public transport corporations. The Telephone and Telegraph Administration (RTT) is also state owned, as is the Regie des Postes. Since the Société Nationale d'Investissments (SNI) was formed in 1962 as a vehicle for state participations, the Government's involvement in industry has increased but the main emphasis is still very much on private industry. In the supply of electricity, for example, only around 2.5 per cent comes from public authorities, the rest being supplied by private utilities, listed above, though mixed public and private utility companies also play a part. The state also runs the Ostend-Dover Line, the cross-channel ferry company started in 1846. The biggest shipping concern is the Compagnie Maritime Belge, in which Société Générale has an interest. Small business still plays a significant part in the Belgian economy with some 800,000 small firms or self-employed people – around one-fifth of the working population – but their number is declining while that of the holding companies, of which probably around a dozen have the lion's share of industrial assets, is increasing. They employ half the country's total workforce and represent 80 per cent of total capital, according to one survey.

With the loss of its Congo interests around 1960, Belgium suffered a severe economic blow which was partly compensated for by its success in the Common Market which became effective about the same time. But perhaps the most important prop to the economy since 1960 has been foreign investment and U.S. investment in particular. The high level of U.S. investment in Belgium has been a point of some concern with other EEC countries, notably Holland and its impact has been proportionately much greater in Belgium than in any other part of the EEC. The investment is concentrated in areas of high technology in the main and one of the major criticisms of the Belgian holding companies in recent years has been their reluctance or inability to close this technology gap themselves. The U.S. multinational companies were able to manoeuvre around the lumbering (if not exactly sleeping) giants of the Belgian industrial scene with relative ease. Nevertheless the key basic industries are still very much the province of the holding companies as has been shown.

Luxembourg

So far as Luxembourg is concerned, to say 'ARBED' (Aciéries Réunies de Burbach-Eich-Dudelange) is virtually to speak for the whole of industry. It is by far the largest company in the Grand Duchy and accounts for 90 per cent of iron and steel production there, 70 per cent of the country's exports, 50 per cent of its total industrial manpower and about 25 or 30 per cent of its gross national product. Its headquarters building is among the most impressive buildings in Luxembourg. The concern is mainly in foreign ownership. The two biggest shareholders are (with 15 per cent each) none other than La Générale of Belgium and the French Schneider group (part of Baron Empain's domain). Turnover is around the equivalent of £750 million a year. The ARBED group is split into several main divisions, the largest being steel, which

includes the ARBED works in Luxembourg, and the Sidmar company
on the Belgian coast. Other divisions produce coal and iron ore as well
as fabrication industries.

Perhaps Luxembourg's most important rôle though, has become that
of a tax haven for multinational concerns. One might for instance turn
up the report of a company like ADELA based in Luxembourg only to
discover that it is a 'multinational private investment company' which
operates in Latin America. If Belgium is the land of the indigenous
industrial holding company then Luxembourg is the country of the
immigrant financial holding company – a sort of sham international
head office where companies maintain the fiction of having their
operational headquarters purely for fiscal convenience. In fact as
Morphologie des Groupes Financiers says, Luxembourg has built up a
veritable *'industrie du holding'* by virtue of uniquely favourable tax
legislation.

*'La législation grand-ducal a instauré un régime fiscal très favorable
pour les 'holding companies' au sens étroit, c'est à dire pour les sociétiés
de participations financières. La domiciliation au Grand-Duché presente
de nets avantages dans le domaine des impôts.'* But the essential point
to remember is just what little part, if any, these fictitious head offices
have in running the companies they provide a base for.

*'La plupart des holdings luxembourgeois ne constituent pas un
centre d'initiative n'apportent pas de concours techniques ou
financiers, ils ne dirigent ni ne contrôlent, ils ne co-ordonnent ni ne
rationaïisent les entreprises dans lesquelles ils détiennent des
participations comme c'est le cas des grandes sociétés financières.'*

CHAPTER 8 IRELAND: THE IMMIGRANT MORTGAGE

Anthony Rowley

When will the day break in Erin; when will her day-star arise?

There is something curiously (and perhaps characteristically) illogical about the structure of Irish industry, though Ireland cannot be entirely blamed for that. The Industrial Revolution did not effectively get under way there until well into the twentieth century and then it was very much a half-hearted affair. During the centuries-long British rule Ireland's economic interests had been often sacrificed to those of Britain, and it was difficult for the newly-founded Irish Republic to begin in the 1920s an industrial revolution which most of her European neighbours had undergone a century or so before. Moreover the ensuing economic war with Britain and a policy of high tariff protection from the rest of the world meant that Ireland was cut off from the markets she badly needed in order to thrive industrially and to grow economically. Though some infant native industries were nurtured behind these tariff walls, most outsiders still think with some justification of Irish industry in terms of a handful of manufactures: whiskey, tobacco, glassware, textiles and carpets.

Grafted onto this limited industrial base now, however, is a whole range of advanced technological skills, all brought in by the immigrant multinational companies which Ireland has done so much to encourage over the past decade. But the solid middle layer of manufacturing industry is largely missing and it is this which gives industry an air of imbalance. Since Ireland joined the EEC it may no longer be so true that 'when England coughs, Ireland catches a cold' yet her economic constitution looks far from robust even now. Any slowing down in world trade could bring in its train a retreat from the multinational activity Ireland is so highly dependent upon.

The Historical Context

Ireland caught only the faintest whiff of the industrial revolution taking place across the Irish Sea in England two centuries ago. In the north of Ireland a fairly modest linen industry sprang up based on indigenous flax and that in turn helped finance the shipbuilding industry for which the North is now well known.* But in the main Ireland continued to drift along unchanged by industrial or social revolution as a predominantly agricultural nation, or as the 'farmyard of England' as Irishmen still put it with a vestigial hint of resentment. The Anglo-Irish (protestant) settlers, the so-called 'Ascendancy' were lords of the land rather than barons of industry.

Virtually no manufacturing industry developed until after the separation from Britain, in the early 1920s. By then a revolution had indeed taken place in Ireland – the 1916 uprising, ostensibly against English rule but in fact more of a social revolution against ruling class structures, which spilled over into the subsequent civil war. Thereafter industries were founded within a relatively democratic framework. Few people had a large fixed capital stake in the economy and factory owners or managers were not expected to lord it over their workers. To this day Irish society remains essentially egalitarian. There is some truth moreover in the suggestion by the Irish playwright Sean O'Casey that if you look closely you will pick out a small red star glimmering against the firmament of Ireland's national green.

The newly formed republican state had to take a hand in building Irish industry during the 1920s, once the 'dead hand' of British policy no longer rested upon the country. One of the ways in which it chose to do this was by setting up a kind of state investment bank, the Industrial Credit Company or *Chairde Tionscail*. The object was to launch and finance a series of Irish companies in key industrial sectors though the founders of the ICC, men like Dr James Beddy, were practical enough to see that Ireland would continue to rely heavily on foreign industry for a long time to come.

They persuaded some of the great British companies to issue shares in separately-quoted Irish subsidiaries so that Irishmen would invest their savings in nominally Irish enterprise. Thus alongside new and essentially Irish enterprises such as Irish Sugar, Irish Tanners, Irish Aluminium, Irish Wire Products, Irish Worsted Mills and so on the decade of the 1920s and early 1930s also saw the ICC handling the share issues of companies like Dunlop (Ireland), Ranks (Ireland) and others like them.[27] The Irish Life, largest of the life assurance companies in Ireland, was also launched around this time as a state-owned enterprise and today gives the Government a stake in a portfolio of industrial shares and other securities worth some £150

---

*Harland and Wolff shipbuilders (in which the British Government has a 48 per cent stake) is Northern Ireland's biggest employer.

million ($360 million.)

Even then however, the rather timid and essentially defensive trade policies followed by successive Irish governments led to protection and the effect was compounded by the economic war with Britain. All this ensured that Ireland's 'emergent' industry hardly emerged at all as an internationally viable entity until some thirty years later. It was not until the late 1950s when Sean Lemass became Prime Minister and began to open up the economy to the outside world that Irish industry developed on any meaningful scale.* Still it was not destined to be the kind of development which would encourage the growth of native industry.

Lemass and his chief economic adviser, Dr Kenneth Whitaker who is now governor of the state-owned Central Bank, saw that like any other developing country Ireland would have to rely on immigrant industry to provide much of its growth. Immigrant multinational companies would bring with them the kind of ready made international markets which Ireland lacked.

Locked in behind protective trade walls, Ireland's own industrialists had failed to develop these markets and their home market consisted of barely three million people, many of whom were unable to afford more than the basic necessities of life. So it was hardly surprising that in many important sectors native industry was either still in its infancy or had failed to get going at all. One consequence was an acute lack of jobs and a continuing high rate of emigration, mainly to Britain. Remitted earnings from Irish emigrants became a major factor in the national economy though this was no source of satisfaction to Irish politicians and others with aspirations towards economic self-sufficiency.

An industrial development programme was set in train through state and quasi-state organisations such as the Industrial Development Authority, the Shannon Free Airport Development Company in the West of Ireland and the Industrial Credit Company. Free trade policies were pursued, including the signing of an important free trade agreement with Britain, and the Irish Export Board was set up. Industrialists were offered tax concessions, financial grants, help with industrial training and other incentives. The whole package was so well planned and successful that it has since been copied by numerous developing countries.

*The first programme for Economic Expansion was published in 1958.

Immigrant Invasion

One of the most important and far-reaching provisions was the exemption of exports from corporate taxes. Though this was aimed equally at home industry and foreign industry in theory, in practice it favoured the immigrant companies as just about all of their output from Ireland was exported anyway. The result was predictable. By the end of March 1973, 799 new industrial projects had been set up in Ireland with the aid of the new incentives (over about ten years) and of these no less than 557 were sponsored by overseas firms and only 242 by Irish manufacturers. They represent a total investment of £317.6 million of which £257.0 million is in foreign-based projects and £60.6 million in Irish firms.

Of the overseas-sponsored firms established in Ireland during the 1960s around 40 per cent were from Britain, 25 per cent from the U.S.A., 20 per cent from West Germany and five per cent from Holland. Others came from Austria, Belgium, Canada, Denmark, Finland, France, Italy, Japan, South Africa, Sweden and Switzerland. Their products include engineering goods, computers, electronics and electrical equipment, pharmaceuticals and chemicals, textiles, food-stuffs, metal and plastic products and leisure goods. The Industrial Development Authority stresses that these immigrant companies have provided a large proportion of the capital for expanding the Irish industrial sector and have introduced new products, modern technologies and modern marketing and management methods. There is certainly no doubt about their impact on the economy. The rate of industrial expansion in the 1960s was very impressive. This expansion was the biggest single element in the 48 per cent increase in gross national product to £1,648 million between 1960 and 1971. Industrial exports (thanks mainly to the tax incentives) rose from £83.8 million to £394.3 million over the same period.

But all this engendered a certain amount of discontent among trades unionists, academics, economists and some politicians in Ireland who claimed that Britain's centuries-long domination of the national economy had simply been replaced by a multinational company hegemony. Trade union leaders now are pressing for more information on the profits and activities of the multinationals in return for their own continuing co-operation in the national wage agreements which make Ireland an even more attractive place to establish a manufacturing base.

Nevertheless it is hard for any of these people to argue too forcibly

Fig. 6 Investment in Industrial Projects in Ireland by the Principal Source Countries as at the end of 1973.

Country	Amount Invested	No. of Projects
	£ (Million)	
Britain	48.1	195
U.S.A.	96.5	149
Germany	20.0	107
Netherlands	39.2	24
Ireland	60.6	242
Others	53.2	82

Source: Industrial Development Authority, Dublin.

against the fact that the industrial development programme, biased as it has proved towards foreign companies, has resulted in higher employment and lower emigration. Some 58,000 jobs were created in the industrial sector during the 1960s (taking manufacturing employment up to around 230,000) and emigration fell from 44,000 in 1960 to under 12,000 in 1970. By the end of 1972 net emigration had virtually ceased for the first time in over a hundred years.

In all this, the main body of native Irish industry has remained highly fragmented, as an official study published in 1972 showed.[28] Small companies predominate. Ninety per cent of the 10,000 native Irish companies are private unquoted ones and 80 per cent of this figure are so-called 'close' companies, controlled by just five or fewer share-holders.

Irish economic history in fact records the emergence of very few well-known industrialists, apart from Arthur Guinness, the founder of Guinnesses Brewery in Dublin in 1759,[29] and Patrick James Carroll, who founded P.J. Carroll's tobacco manufactory at Dundalk in 1824. Earlier this century there was William Martin Murphy, the 'Bantry Jobber' as James Joyce called him in *Ulysses*, who achieved fame or infamy, depending on which way you look at it, through his stubborn opposition to Big Jim Larkin's trade union activities at the time of the 1913 strike and lockout in Dublin. Murphy at one time owned the Dublin United Tramway Company (since nationalised) as well as interests in British tramway systems, and department stores and hotels. He also had interests in North Africa but his industrial empire has long since crumbled.

The Irish Industrialist

If history has produced a special sort of industrial structure in Ireland it has also produced a special sort of contemporary industrialist. One such is Donal Carroll, chairman of P.J. Carroll and much more of a Kennedy-style democrat than an industrial autocrat. He is a singular man, a banker-industrialist in the Continental tradition yet far removed from the caricature picture of a fat, cigar-smoking tycoon this normally conjures up. He is an idealist almost to the point of naivety on occasions.

The continually recurring theme in his conversation is the need to reconcile wider interests than those which an industrialist normally concerns himself with. It is no longer possible to regard an optimum return on capital as the highest priority in industry, he maintains. Some recognition is needed of the social forces involved. The old distinctions between the rights of capital and those of labour are breaking down.

Admittedly all this foreshadows the general move towards a fundamental re-appraisal and reform of company law in Britain and elsewhere at present. But the Carrolls have anticipated these reforms by introducing something they call 'one-class employment' into P.J. Carrolls. This is an attempt to relate effort to reward uniformly throughout the company so that everyone, from the managing director to line operators, is paid strictly according to the effort they put in. If anything the system favours the manual workers rather than the white collar staff and executives — a point Donal Carroll likes to emphasise. A special 'monotony factor' is built into the pay equation for manual grades to compensate them for lack of mental stimulation in certain tasks.

Carrolls have also abolished the traditional distinction between workers and staff by offering them all similar conditions and terms of employment. These old distinctions were socially divisive and absolute anathema to Donal Carroll's philosophies of reconciliation. He has a vision of a new industrial order based on fair treatment and participation, and quotes David Rockefeller as the prophet of this order. In his admiration of that which is best in the American business ethic, Donal Carroll is by no means alone among Irishmen. Broadly speaking America stands for an open society as they see it, and Britain for a closed one.

In one important respect Carrolls itself has changed from a closed to an open society, in that most sensitive area for Ireland, religious toleration. The company was formerly reputed to employ Catholics only, an understandable counter perhaps to the Protestant domination of business when Carrolls was founded. Now Donal Carroll says he doubts whether any but a few employees would know or care what religious denomination their colleagues belong to. This seems to be true of other leading Irish industrial companies too. Directors do not like to talk about the subject but if pressed will admit that the problem of religious prejudices once loomed fairly large until professionalism and internationalism became the key to managerial success, regardless of creed.

In 1970 a somewhat bizarre supermerger was proposed in Ireland. For a short time it looked as though the half dozen most powerful families in industry there would join forces. The man behind this projected supermerger was none other than Donal Carroll. At his instigation P.J. Carroll, Waterford Glass, Irish Glass Bottle and United Distillers (already an amalgam of powerful family interests) began to talk of joint marketing which was to be followed ultimately by a complete merger of interests. They announced the scheme to an astonished stock exchange in Dublin and an equally surprised City of London. The idea was a bold one even by British standards of takeover and merger. But after a decent interval to allow the excitement to die down the scheme was quietly dropped. Just why it was shelved has never been fully explained. Donal Carroll said that it was a 'national visionary concept' but that it foundered because of managerial problems. He has tried to go too far and too fast for many people's liking. After steering Lloyds and Bolsa International Bank through the turbid waters of a merger he pulled out in 1973, seemingly because his zeal for reform was not matched by that of Lloyds, the dominant partner.

At the time the supermerger was proposed United Distillers represented a still new and uneasy alliance among three famous Irish families whose names are synonomous with whiskey or other drinks. They are Murphy, of Cork Distillers, Jameson and Power. For them to have become part of a vast holding company might have helped smooth the path of their own union. Although they did not accept Carroll's master-scheme at least they agreed to accept one of his former executives, Kevin McCourt, as managing director to keep the peace among them. All three families had for years fought among themselves for control of the Irish whiskey market until a more powerful and common enemy, the Scottish whisky industry, appeared likely to crush them all after the Anglo-Irish free trade agreement was signed in the mid 1960s. Entry into Europe was coming closer too, it seemed at the time, so the Irish whiskey barons agreed to end their feuding. Their sales and profits have since trebled.

However, United Distillers (subsequently restyled 'Irish Distillers') had to allow Seagram of Canada, reputedly the world's biggest distiller, to take a 15 per cent stake in the group as the price for access to the North American market. And P.J. Carroll has sold a 40 per cent stake to Rothmans International. Multinational giants like these usually like to control their associate companies eventually and to turn them into subsidiaries. Irish industry remains singularly devoid of government protection against outside takeovers of this kind and Donal Carroll may well have foreseen the dangers when he suggested the (defensive?) supermerger.

Another prospective party to that merger was Patrick McGrath, a

close friend of Donal Carroll and one of the more colourful figures in
Irish industry. He is an elusive figure, shunning publicity and reputed to
be among the richest men in Ireland if not *the* richest. He is head of
both Waterford Glass and Irish Glass Bottle and, like Lord Iveagh of
Guinness, is a Senator of the Irish Republic.

The McGrath empire has its roots in the Irish Sweepstakes — an
honourable pedigree for an Irish enterprise — founded in the early
1930s by Patrick McGrath's father Joe along with a Dublin bookmaker,
Dick Duggan, and a British Army officer, Captain Spencer Freeman.
They founded the Irish Hospital Sweepstakes Company, a lottery which
donates part of its proceeds to hospitals while raising a good deal of
money for its promoters through a commission or percentage on tickets
sold. It is nowadays known simply as the 'Hospitals Trust' and Patrick
McGrathis both chairman and managing director. His father employed
some of the money made from the sweepstakes to buy into Irish Glass
Bottle and it was he who was largely responsible for reviving the
Waterford glass industry now world-renowned for its exquisite crystal
glassware. Waterford is in fact a separately quoted company and a very
popular share on the Irish stock market. Patrick McGrath has taken
over the reins of the business empire his father founded while his
brother Seamus has become best known as a horse owner and trainer.
Patrick is also chairman of Celtic Oil, a company formed to search for
oil and gas in the sea off Waterford and Cork. Celtic has not yet had
any real success but Ireland continues to hope for new riches from the
sea just as it hopes for a mineral mining boom from Tara.

The Entrepreneurs

Tara is the mineral find which a couple of years ago led to seething
stock market speculation about a mining boom of Klondike pro-
portions for Ireland. Tara Exploration is in fact a Canadian registered
company but controlled by four Irishmen, Pat Hughes (Ireland's 'Mr
Mining'), Michael McCarthy, Mat Gilroy and Joe McParland. All four
emigrated from Ireland (though only McCarthy from the Republic, the
rest being from the North of Ireland) to Toronto in Canada to work as
builders' labourers. From there they found their way to Uranium City
in Saskatchewan where they did some small-time, though successful,
prospecting for ores.

Then, acting on Pat Hughes' conviction that there were mineral
riches to be found back home in their native Ireland the four began

'commuting' back there to prospect. They struck zinc at Tynagh in County Galway in the early 1960s and used the earnings from Tynagh to prospect for bigger things. They found them at Navan some thirty miles north-west of Dublin, in the shape of an apparently enormous body of lead and zinc ore, now known as Tara. If the find proves as good as initial indications suggest, and if Tara Exploration can overcome the fearsome legal complications it seems to have run into in exploiting its find, then it will mine and refine the ores from Navan and make a lot of money in the process. Inevitably there have been pressures for nationalisation of these newly discovered riches and the tax holiday offered by the Government to mining prospectors has been dropped in order to maximise state revenues.

One of the major shareholders in Tara was for a time Tony O'Reilly,* the golden boy of Irish business, one of the new young Catholic entrepreneurs who seem to be making so much of the running just now. Six feet tall and with flaming red hair, O'Reilly raced to fame first across the rugby field as a member of the British Lions team and then across the firmament of Irish business. He is a leader of that growing band of Irishmen, who as one Dublin banker put it, have nowhere to go but up, and are prepared to fight hard to get there.

He began at the Allied Irish Investment Bank, merchant banking arm of the Allied Bank. Together with two other Allied men, Vincent Ferguson and Nicholas Leonard, O'Reilly pulled off a series of financial deals which culminated in the formation of his own investment company, Fitzwilliam Securities. The Ulster Bank, from where O'Reilly obtained much of his initial funds and of which he is now a director, took a stake in Fitzwilliam.

In turn Fitzwilliam went on to buy up a rather sleepy old drapery company, Crowe Wilson, which was quoted on the Stock Exchange. It was a typical 'shell' company operation. Once the word got round that O'Reilly had acquired control of Crowe Wilson its shares began to rise on the stock market. Taking advantage of their enhanced value O'Reilly then proceeded to exchange these shares to force shares in other companies he wanted to buy. Thus he was able to 'inject' other interests, such as pharmaceuticals, building operations and wines and spirits retailing, into Crowe Wilson and to turn it into an industrial

---

*He later sold out to the Canadian mining group 'Cominco' which together with Charter Consolidated, the mining finance house, and associates now holds 31 per cent of Tara.

conglomerate.

The grand coup for O'Reilly came later however when he succeeded in taking over W.& H.M. Goulding, the Irish fertiliser concern in 1972, and amalgamating it with Fitzwilliam and Crowe Wilson. It was really a reverse takeover as Gouldings was much bigger than the O'Reilly interests, so they 'reversed into Gouldings' to use the stock market jargon. At a stroke this move gave O'Reilly solid asset backing for his business enterprises and solid respectability in financial and investment circles. The amalgam of all these interests was renamed 'Fitzwilton', a holding company with very wide interests.

Gouldings had been run by Sir Basil Goulding, a distinctly aristocratic figure in Irish business (an old Wykehamist and Oxford man), with the delightfully idiosyncratic tendency to write his annual report to shareholders in rhyming couplets – or part of it at least. One of his aphorisms which emphasise his disdain for the financial aspect of business was that: 'the understanding of taxation and the computation of it are not things given to ordinary mortals.' Sir Basil was made chairman of Fitzwilton. There were many who doubted whether this improbable merger of interests between the rather aristocratic patron of the arts, Goulding, and the thrusting young tycoon, O'Reilly, would work out – so far it appears to have done so.

O'Reilly has himself acquired something of an Establishment image nowadays. Through his association with Erin Foods (food processing offshoot of the state-owned Irish Sugar Company) he was noticed by H.J. Heinz the American food giant which has a joint subsidiary with Erin. Heinz signed up O'Reilly and his rise there was meteoric. He became vice-president then world-wide president of the whole concern. Since then he has been a strong advocate of multinational enterprise and (equally predictably) he has been castigated by the left wing Sinn Fein party for taking such a heretical line.

O'Reilly has also acquired an image of gracious living for himself. He bought a splendid Georgian mansion at the Curragh (site of the famous racecourse) near Dublin for some £200,000. He recently bought control of the *Irish Independent* newspaper group once owned by William Martin Murphy. By linking the two names together, some commentators were heard to say at the time that history was repeating itself.

Jefferson Smurfit is not only a well-known name in Irish industry, it is an unusual name for an unusual man. Jefferson Smurfit started life as a tailor's apprentice in the north of England (he is of Irish parentage) and then went on to acquire a chain of outfitters shops. Clothes rationing in Britain during the last war, plus the fact that most men were in uniform at the time anyway, killed his business but another business he had quite reluctanty acquired was to prove his remaking. This was a tiny box-making concern in Dublin bought strictly as a favour for about £300 from the priest who married Smurfit. Smurfit hoped the priest would refuse such a derisory offer but he didn't. The business prospered and today it is one of the largest packaging concerns in Europe and makes profits of around £3 million a year — 10,000 times what Smurfit paid for it.

Guinnesses

What of Guinness, it might be asked at this late stage in a chapter on Irish industry. The answer is that while Ireland might not be Ireland without Guinness, the reverse does not really apply any longer. The headquarters of the now multinational Guinness group has been in London since the end of the nineteenth century. Though the original Guinness brewery was founded in Dublin in 1759 at St James's Gate, Guinness became a quoted company on the London Stock Exchange as early as 1886 when Ireland was still part of Britain. After the separation of the two countries in 1922 Guinness decided to stay where the big market was so far as raising finance was concerned and made its headquarters in London.

When it was decided to build a second Guinness brewery to supply the home markets in the 1930s, the site chosen for this was at Park Royal in north-west London. Later there was talk of whether the Irish operation could remain viable, to the horror of Dubliners who regard St James's Gate still as the true home of Guinness. At present some £20 million is having to be spent on modernising the Irish brewery. Questions about whether Guinness is really Irish or English look rather academic however beside the simple statistic that more Guinness is now brewed on the Equator in Nigeria and Malaya than in Europe.

The merchant-banking Guinnesses of Guinness & Mahon (now Guinness Peat) have long been a separate scion of the main line Guinnesses, though one of them, A.P.B. Guinness, is on the board of Arthur Guinness, Son & Company, the main publically-quoted holding company. Its chairman is the present Arthur Guinness, 3rd Earl of Iveagh. A vice-chairman of the group is Lord Moyne (Bryan Walter Guinness whose eldest son Jonathon, was the controversial chairman of the right wing 'Monday Club' in British Tory politics) though Lord

Moyne is perhaps better known as a poet, playwright and novelist.

The Future

These are some of the best-known names in Irish industry and a fairly limited range of industry it is though there are one or two other prosperous sectors including construction (Cement Roadstone and Abbey Group being two of the biggest there) and carpets (Youghal) as well as textiles. It is hard to find continuity in the way these business empires have developed or in attitudes towards running them. Nor is there any sign yet of a coherent plan for the future development of native industry. In its industrial structure Ireland is in some ways more akin to a South-East Asia republic like Singapore or Taiwan – an offshore base for multinational enterprise – than a modern western industrial state.

Like its British counterpart (with which it is now federated) the Irish Stock Exchange has seen some hectic takeover and merger activity in recent times. The effect of this has been to reshuffle the ownership of existing companies but has not added to the overall industrial asset base. Any move now to build up an infrastructure of Irish-owned basic and advanced manufacturing industry – steel, motor vehicles, ship-building, engineering, electronics, chemicals, pharmaceuticals etc – would require a great deal of time and a massive injection of capital. It might be politically unpopular too because of the drain on national resources.

It is difficult to see how the state could extend its influence into these spheres without antagonising immigrant industry on which Ireland relies so heavily for jobs and markets. There is little by way of state-owned industry at present apart from the national airline, Aer Lingus, the public transport body CIE, the electricity authority ESB, B+I the Irish Sea shipping line and Bord Na Mona the peat authority. As a short-term expedient, the policy of encouraging immigrant industry has worked very well but it could be that Ireland has mortgaged a good part of its long-term industrial future to this policy.

CHAPTER 9 DENMARK: ECONOMIC DEMOCRACY OR CRISIS?

Anthony Rowley & Peter Rosendahl

Denmark has a unique industrial structure within the EEC and one which is little known outside the country. Few of the big and well-known names in Scandinavian industry belong to Denmark. Sweden can boast of Volvo, Saab, Swedish Match and L.M. Ericsson and Norway of Borregaard, Tandberg and Norsk Hydro but the two mentions that Denmark rates among the top twenty Scandinavian companies are relatively obscure in the world of international business. They seem deliberately to have courted obscurity. Yet in terms of relative size, names like the Maersk group and the East Asiatic Company (Ost Asiatiske Kompagni) stand out like twin pinnacles among the myriad foothills of Danish industry. Denmark may not have its Rothschilds or anything like the legendary Wallenburg dynasty in Sweden (heirs to the old Kruger industrial empire) but in dynastic terms one name must stand out against all others. It is that of Arnold Maersk Mc-Kinney Møller, head of Maersk and the biggest shipowner in Europe. Powerful as he is however, it would be wrong to talk of Danish industry in dynastic terms. It is more a country of small family proprietorship where the craft tradition is giving way only slowly to big business and one where capitalism seems to coexist very uneasily with socialism.

It is difficult to see Maersk and East Asiatic in perspective or to understand the evolution towards a unique kind of 'economic democracy' in Denmark without viewing them against the historical background. Traditionally an agricultural nation, Denmark had no basic raw materials to fuel and early industrial revolution or capital to finance it. The Industrial Revolution, if such it can be called, did not arrive until the late 1950s. The big exceptions were, of course, the Viking tradition of shipbuilding and Denmark's adventures in international trading, activities which still live on and which significantly form the bedrock of the Maersk and Ost Asiatiske empires.

Unlike Sweden, Denmark had virtually no reserves of indigenous iron and developed no tradition of smelting it. The matrix of a primary industrial revolution was absent and even today most industry is based on secondary manufacture from imported raw materials. However the predominance of agriculture did give rise to an important food-processing industry and today several of the more internationally known Danish companies, such as the United Breweries, Carlsberg and Tuborg, as well as Plumrose the canned meat group still have their roots in agricultural production.

Revolution or Evolution?

Denmark's Industrial Revolution, when it finally did come, was really more a speeding up of the process of evolution. There had been a constant drift from the land, but it accelerated in the post-war years and jobs in industry had to be provided in order to compensate. Denmark had to find a suitable niche where it could compete with international industry and chose to do so partly by specialising in components and sub-assemblies for other countries' products – such as parts for IBM computers, assemblies for the MERV rocket, and ships radios. As one Danish commentator put it: 'The Danes are a nation of sub-contractors.'

They are also a nation of craftsmen. Manual crafts have not died out with the growth of manufacturing industry as it was believed they would. At the start of the 1970s there were 75,000 craft trade establishments in Denmark employing 400,000 people in total and contributing 19 per cent of the national product as against 19.5 per cent for industry. No less than 79 per cent of the total industrial undertakings in Denmark employ 10 people or under and a further 14 per cent employ between 10 and 20. Joint stock companies employing between 20 and 50 people make up only 2 per cent of the total and those with over fifty employees a further 2 per cent.[30]

Nevertheless if the traditional craft trades still invoke more loyalty among Danes than do the big industrial corporations the growth of larger-scale industry has become more pronounced during the past twenty years. As the Official Handbook on Denmark[31] says:

'The really decisive development (in manufacturing industry) has taken place since 1957, strongly influenced by world trends and the liberalisation of trade which has enabled Danish industry to operate at an entirely different, specialised level in a wider market than before. Since 1957 Danish industry has become internationally minded, the mainstay of the economy and the Danish nation's expansive potential for the future.'

Significantly it was in the expansionist world trade climate of the late

1950s and 1960s that Scandinavia's general industrial expansion was engendered (though Sweden had a headstart) as well as that of Denmark's new partner in the EEC, Ireland. If there is now to be a slowing down in the growth of world trade, as seemed likely even before the international oil crisis and which now appears inevitable, Denmark's membership of the EEC will be vital to her economic survival as an industrial nation. The EEC looks like providing the sort of fresh impetus to Danish growth that Efta (the European Free Trade Association) and Nordek (the Scandinavian common market) provided in the past.

Meanwhile the size of Denmark's industrial units will probably have to grow in order to make them internationally competitive even within Europe. Already many of the small craft and manufacturing units have begun to band together on the same site to share common facilities. But one of the big restrictions on growth, apart from the shortage of raw materials, looks like being a lack of capital for industrial expansion. There has been a decline in the degree of self financing in industry and a much greater reliance on bank borrowing. Only a small proportion of new industrial finance has been raised by increasing share capital because of the Dane's traditional reserve about this form of investment. The Copenhagen Stock Exchange (Københavns Fondsbørs) – the only one in the country – is not the most popular institution in Danish national life.

'Economic Democracy'

Against this background it is easier to understand the revolutionary moves towards 'economic democracy' which the Social Democratic Party made in 1973. The controversy surrounding these proposals finally helped bring down the Social Democrat government in Denmark at the end of 1973 after they had been almost continuously in office for a quarter of a century. The minority Liberal government which took over in December 1973 and which governs with the aid of the Conservatives has since shelved the proposals for economic democracy and replaced them with watered-down plans for worker participation in the running of industry. But many Danes regard the more radical proposals as being simply 'on ice', to be thawed out and implemented once the Social Democrats return to power.

Danes are fiercely egalitarian and against any form of class structure, even the distinction between workers and shareholders in industry. The principle behind the plans for economic democracy was to take the ownership of industry out of the hands of shareholders, which means mainly private families and the banks in the context of Denmark, and to put it firmly in the hands of the workers by state direction.

This was to be achieved through the instrument of two Bills introduced in 1973, one by the Minister of Labour, on the right of co-ownership of employees, and the other by the Minister of Commerce, on the right of co-determination in joint stock companies. The three officially stated aims were: first, to 'assure the employees a reasonable share of the capital growth which will take place in Danish society in the years to come.' Secondly, to 'strengthen the right of co-determination through an increased say in the management (board) of the undertaking where they work.' Thirdly, to 'contribute to an increase in future capital formation with the purpose of promoting investments in economic life and thus establish a better basis of full employment, a rise in living standards and greater social progress.'

This rather splendid-sounding revolution in the ownership of industry was to be achieved through the medium of an 'Employees' Investment and Dividend Fund' to be managed by a council of 60 members – 36 appointed by employee organisations (trade unions in the main) and 24 by the Minister of Labour. The employers would thus have had a minority say. All employers in Denmark, whether private or public companies, would have to contribute annually a sum equal to half a per cent of their total wages and salaries bill to the fund, rising to 5 per cent in 1983. The contribution was not to be made out of wages but from firms' other resources and there was a prospect of their having to make an additional contribution from profits in time.

Most joint stock and private companies were given the option of making up to two-thirds of their contribution to the fund in the shape of equity shares (this was mandatory for the largest companies) which automatically would have rendered the fund a major shareholder in all companies over a period of time. As the fund would have belonged to the workers they would ultimately have become the biggest single owners of industry, though it was laid down that 'employee capital cannot be increased beyond 50 per cent of the total share capital of each company.' That part of the contribution made in cash was to enable the fund to buy shares in any company it chose or to make loans – either way strengthening its hold on industry. The administration of the loan system was to be left to the banks and savings banks.

All employees within the scheme would be issued with certificates – certificates of shareholding in effect though these could not be negotiated or borrowed on. However, after seven years the employee had the right to draw the value of the certificate including dividend and interest credits.

The overall object was to foster industrial investment in a national context which the authors of the Bills evidently assumed that private enterprise was incapable of doing. Critics of the proposals – and there was no shortage of them among employers as well as some employees – said that funds would be used for propping up inefficient industry in order to maintain full employment and in any case the Fund would be arbitrarily and inexpertly administered. The Government countered by saying that: 'To ensure the employees' ability to exercise these rights (of managing the fund) in the best possible way, the Fund will undertake an educational and informative activity and grant assistance as to managerial economy and accounts.' Opposition to the proposals eventually reached a crescendo and helped to precipitate the defeat of the Social Democrats at the polls. But the Opposition nevertheless felt bound to introduce proposals of their own for worker participation in management, stopping short nevertheless of worker control.

East Asiatic Company – EAC or ØK as it is usually known – was among the more vocal critics of the plans for economic democracy. In its 1973 annual report to shareholders the company said: 'Business life is threatened by interferences in conditions which are managed best under voluntary terms.' Other companies attacked the plans in similar vein and alleged the Government's policy to be 'hostile to business life.' Often the business community referred to the plans for economic democracy as calculated to scare off Norwegian and Swedish companies from investing in Denmark after they had planned to do so once Denmark joined the EEC. Economic democracy was also attacked on the grounds that it discouraged capital investment by Danish industrialists in their own country.

The Old Trading Empires

EAC introduced its own employee share scheme and this was widely seen as a counter to the former Prime Minister Anker Jorgensen's scheme for economic democracy. Nowadays some 24 million Kroner of the shares in EAC – around 5 per cent of the total – are owned by the employees of the group. Everyone who has worked with the parent company for more than one year is allowed to buy shares up to the

value of several thousand Kroner at a favourable price. The holdings of
those employees who over a period have made maximum use of this
facility today stands at around 15,000 Kroner or around £1,000.

The history of the East Asiatic Company in many ways resembles
that of A.P. Møller (Maersk). Both started as shipping companies and
EAC was mainly concerned with the transportation of teak wood from
plantations in Thailand. Denmark has long-standing connections with
Thailand, one of the most recent manifestations of which was the
launching aid given by the joint Scandinavian airline, SAS, to the
emergent Thai International airlines. Since it was founded in 1897 EAC
has grown into an international business giant, owning and controlling
more than 150 companies in six continents and with a turnover in
excess of £1,000 million equivalent.

East Asiatic and A.P. Møller are the best examples of how the
dynasties created on the basis of an old Danish trade – shipping – have
learned to adapt and to participate in the country's conversion to
post-war industrial life. Their early start in their respective fields gave
them a clear lead over later competitors and their international
connections have made them influential enough to be largely beyond
the pale of Danish Government interference. Through their international trading connections too they have built up formidable capital
reserves which they could invest back home in Denmark, putting them
at a tremendous advantage over domestic-based groups in what is still
an embryo capital market by international standards.

Though trading and shipping are still the main lines of business at
East Asiatic its activities extend into pharmaceutical production,
brewing (Carlsberg), rubber extraction, timber production, engineering
manufacture, palm oil production and many other areas just about all
over the world, though with a bias towards the Far East that again
emphasises the old trading links. Its technique has been to approach
Danish and foreign companies with the argument that it has connections
all over the world and the money to market their products. The result is
often a joint venture or a straight takeover by EAC which further
enhances its image as an international holding company – a concept
otherwise alien to Denmark. EAC's best-known interests in Denmark
itself include the Nakskov shipyard and the food manufacturing
concern, Beauvais-Plumrose, which is one of the biggest industrial
corporations in Denmark.

If East Asiatic is known for its corporate image, Maersk is best
known for that of its founder, A.P. Møller, whose son Arnold is now
in charge of the family empire. The roots of the empire go back to

1904 when A.P. Møller joined the shipping company C.K. Hansen at the age of twenty-eight and from there went on to found his own shipping company with a share capital of £10,000. Of this, £1,000 was his own savings and his shipmaster father subscribed a similar amount. The rest of the share capital was subscribed by people in the provincial town of Svendborg on Fuen where Møller lived. That led to the formation of the present parent company of the Maersk empire, the steamship company Svendborg. This is one of the two quoted vehicles through which Maersk is now represented on the Copenhagen Stock Exchange, the other being the Steamship Company of 1912. Svendborg bought its first ship – a 2,000-ton steamer – from a Welsh yard and since then the Maersk fleet has grown to 90 vessels, the biggest of which are supertankers in the 330,000-ton class. Maersk now builds its own ships, the best known of its industrial activities being the Odense Shipyard at Lindoe on Fuen.

More than 90 per cent of the group's earnings still come from shipping and shipbuilding but Maersk also owns 25 industrial concerns. Again like EAC, Møller realised that with the money he made from shipping he could buy into Danish business which he did to the extent of extending his interests over steel, rubber, chemicals, electronics, computers, building materials, air travel (Maersk Air), travel agencies and hypermarkets as well as into sugar production in Tanganyika.

Inevitably the Maersk group is involved in offshore oil and gas exploration too. Its subsidiary Dansk Boreselskab is drilling together with Gulf, Shell, Chevron and Texaco – the DUC consortium – in the Danish 'Dan' field of the North Sea. The Danish Underground Consortium holds the exclusive right to the Danish sector of the North Sea. It is still hoped, despite initial disappointments, that gas and oil discoveries will solve most of Denmark's energy problems.

Maersk's role in the Danish offshore programme began only ten years ago, though the search for oil there started as far back as 1935 when an American company began sporadic drilling. They obtained a concession on whatever they found and that aroused the interest of Gulf Oil which brought the entire share capital in 1938. In the following twenty years Gulf spent over £5 million on the search without finding a single drop of oil, so they left the scene. Exxon (Esso) has since spent a further £1.5 million in exploration though, with similarly poor results.

However, when gas was discovered at Groningen in Holland in 1959 interest in the North Sea intensified. Several German companies began drilling in the German sector and tried to obtain a concession on Danish territories. This was when Maersk began to 'smell oil'. The Danish Government did not expect dramatic results from the new drillings and so Maersk got its concession on very favourable terms. The exploration was to be free of charge and the extraction duty (if any oil were found) only 8.5 per cent — half the incidence that Norway demanded.

After Maersk won his concession the Continental Shelf case followed, ending at the International Court in the Haig. The Germans were claiming a larger area of the Continental Shelf and were ultimately granted it by the court. A.P. Møller were dismayed at this finding and countered it by announcing some findings in part of the North Sea which they were now supposed to cede to the Germans. This galvanised the Danish Government into action and a hectic round of diplomatic activity followed, resulting in a new border line which left the area in question to Denmark after all. Thus the Danish company kept the richest area and even got the concession on that part of the North Sea territory ceded to Germany.

The so-called 'battle of the Shelf' brought the oil search to an end for several years and during this time there was rising anxiety in the House of Maersk. It had been a condition of the original concession from the Danish Government that it could run for fifty years provided that extraction of either oil or gas had started within ten years. The question now was whether Maersk could meet that deadline. Maersk claimed to the Government that it would be a case of *force majeure* if he could not meet it, owing to the Shelf case. This claim was met with a good deal of hostility in the more Left-oriented political circles of Denmark but such is the power of the House of Maersk that it won the day once again and was granted an extension over the original agreement. Work continued and at the beginning of the 1970s the first shipload of oil was brought in to Stignaes refinery on the south-west coast of Zealand. North Sea oil so far amounts to practically nothing compared to Denmark's total consumption of 20 million metric tons a year but drilling there has given Maersk the knowledge to drill in other parts of the world.

Arnold Maersk Mc-Kinney Møller is chairman of the trust created by his father before he died to be repository for shares in Svendborg and the Steamship Company of 1912. Just how large a percentage of those shares Maersk Mc-Kinney owns personally is unknown but stockbrokers in Denmark guess at around 10 per cent of the total capital with a paper worth of 365 million Kroner or more than £25 million. As chairman of the main board Maersk Mc-Kinney has virtually absolute control of A.P. Møller. He is a man who shuns publicity and who is as austere as he is secretive. He was brought up to believe that any employee in the family company was equal to him in prestige and must be treated with respect, a tradition the company continues to honour and it is said that Maersk Mc-Kinney's door is always open to any employee who wants to see him. His austerity shows itself in the lack of ostentation in his office at the group's Copenhagen headquarters and little idiosyncrasies such as his insistence on having replies to messages he sends on the same piece of paper — to save money as well as time. If Maersk Mc-Kinney is travelling on his private plane, his cousin George Andersen (a nephew of A.P. Møller the dynastic founder and a trustee of the family share fund) never travels with him. Like royalty, the two men never expose themselves to the same potential risks.

The one other family dynasty situation worthy of mention in the context of Danish industry is that of F.L. Smidth, the cement plant manufacturer and one of the country's biggest industrial concerns. Smidth is the parent company of the FLS group which has 22,000 employees at 50 factories and which exports to 94 countries. Most of the shares in the group, which was founded in 1882, still belong to three families, Foss, Larsen and Smidth. Nils Foss, successor to one of the original owners is managing director but otherwise the board is made up of professional outsiders, including the chairman, Niels Arnth Jensen former chairman of the Danish Industrial Council.

Beyond the Dynasties

East Asiatic, Maersk and Smidth have been described at some length because they are singular situations. There are other important companies such as Burmeister and Wain the engine makers, Christiani and Nielsen the engineering contracting group, Superfos Chemicals Danfoss the process control group, Hoejgaard, Schultz, Kampsax, Monberg and Thorsen but at this point the pyramid of the Danish industrial structure quickly begins to broaden out from the apex of international-sized companies to the base of purely domestic concerns. There is only one place where Danish engineering concerns really count for anything in terms of international size and that is Greenland where several of the companies mentioned above participate in an engineering and supply company called Danish Arctic Contractors. In the end the two main poles around which most industrial power and influence revolves are EAC and Maersk.

However a great deal has happened within Danish industry over the past twenty years and that is hardly likely to be the end of the story. The open question is whether industry will develop increasingly under the aegis of the state, as the Social Democrats would like, or whether the Liberals and Conservatives will be able to hang onto power long enough to give free enterprise a freer rein. In that case, the Copenhagen Stock Exchange, which has experienced something of a renaissance since it was opened up to outside investors when Denmark joined the EEC, might become a focal point in industrial ownership. There has been a good deal of criticism of the Social Democrats on the grounds that they overspent on the public sector at the expense of the balance of payments and have brought the country to the brink of an economic crisis. There is probably some political hysteria in this claim but even so it could well be that there will be a compensating switch of natural resources into helping the private sector and that Denmark will become increasingly a country of large industrial enterprise rather than modest scale craft trade dominated by a handful of industrial giants.

CHAPTER 10 THE NINE STYLES OF EUROPEAN CAPITALISM

Anthony Rowley

The fact which emerges most strongly from this survey of European industry is that the formation of the EEC sixteen years ago has done virtually nothing to impose uniformity on national systems in the vital area of ownership and control, despite all the harmonising zeal of Brussels. Nor, as was suggested at the outset, has the spread of U.S. multinational business corporations across Europe had any marked impact upon national business life. In West Germany the industry which rose again to perform the post-war economic miracle in many ways resembles the pre-war structure and many of the old controlling trusts, though broken up after the War, re-emerged later in slightly different form but often under the same people. Italian industry, dominated as it is by the parastatal corporations (the biggest of which, IRI, came into being under Mussolini) bears the imprint still of a fascist economic system.* French industry wears a mask of modernity, but behind it whole areas of business remain just as they were fifty years ago, and many people attribute France's recent economic success to the traditional *dirigiste* management of the nation's affairs rather than to the latter-day emergence of the 'efficient, grey business corporations'. In Belgium industry is dominated still by the holding companies and by the Société Générale in particular whose roots go deep into the country's economic history. In Holland the industrial structure mirrors the almost incestuous system of power in politics and other spheres of national life while Denmark's industrial structure is unique within the EEC. In Britain the face of industry has changed a good deal over the past decade but if anything in a manner which removes it even further from the Continental tradition of tight and narrowly held control. Not even Irish industry resembles closely that in Britain though so much of the two countries' economic histories were bound up within one kingdom.

The question that arises in the light of these firmly entrenched national differences is whether the EEC's plans to produce common industrial structures and capital markets within the Community and to

*The economic aspects of facism are essentially the retention of private enterprise but under the rigid control of the state

148

foster mergers across national frontiers are realistic or whether they are doomed to failure from the outset. There was after all the famous, or infamous, precedent of the plan for economic and monetary union which, in failing to take account of the fundamental differences in national economic systems, set up some severe strains within the Community. The other question is whether the nine nations now bound together, however tenuously, within the framework of the EEC can usefully borrow from each other's industrial traditions.

It seems to have been assumed by the functionaries (if not specifically by the architects) of the EEC that Europe is in some way deficient in its provision of capital for industry. This is hardly supported by the facts, as this book shows. In France companies have slight recourse to the international capital markets, preferring instead to rely on domestic bond finance, which they can undertake *en-groupe* for cheapness. In Italy those companies which do not come under the state's financial umbrella can turn either to the banks or to the powerful families that control them. In Germany tne banks are the major source of industry finance and indeed they consider it a duty to ensure the orderly growth of the economy by providing this service. In Belgium it is the holding companies, which are often banking as well as industrial giants, that are the main providers of finance. Danish industry is largely bank financed too. There is little evidence that industry has outgrown its capital markets in these countries and where it occasionally needs exceptional finance it can, and does, turn to the Eurodollar markets. It is difficult to see how one common capital market could cater for all these different traditions of industry finance.

Britain's system of industry finance is again quite different to the others in the EEC and something which can be said with relative certainty is that the wider spread of shareholding along British lines in Europe now looks much less probable. This again has implications for London's ambitions to become the capital market centre of Europe. Continentals have become disenchanted with some aspects of the British system, such as the ease with which speculators can play the takeover game. Never would the French, for instance, allow a 'City' of Paris such freedom as the City is allowed in London, as Rupert Cornwell says. The principle of 'democratic capitalism' in Britain is under attack. Meanwhile what has been seen in Britain as the Continental vice of bank and holding company domination of industry is being viewed afresh as a possible virtue. It is true, as this book has shown, that the holding companies do, as their name implies, exert a tight hold over their subsidiaries in Belgium; the German bankers do sit on the boards of and help to manage the affairs of the companies they invest in; the French *banques d'affaires* do actually help run the companies where they have equity holdings, and the Italian parastatal bodies keep their subsidiaries on a firm rein. But while some think that to acknowledge this is tantamount to condoning dangerous concentrations of power in the Continental system others are now seeing it as a source of strength and continuity in the development of European industry. This indeed seems to be one area where the British could usefully borrow from the Continental tradition instead of vice versa.

Evidently, until the spring of 1974 at least, the EEC Commission in Brussels did not realise how free and rapid the operations of the British capital market can be as they affect industry. Guest, Keen & Nettlefolds the engineers were about to make an unwelcome takeover bid for steel stockholders Miles Druce. Miles Druce asked the Commission to intervene under Coal and Steel Community rules, which it did though apparently in ignorance of the fact that British bids are slipped through in a matter of weeks while share prices are right instead of being carefully scrutinised for months as they are on the Continent. The bid nearly went through by default because of this, though in the event it was allowed anyway.

In the early part of 1974 the Commission was given formal powers by the EEC to scrutinise any bid which would create a grouping with a turnover of £200 million a year equivalent. This measure could have had a dramatic impact on the late 1960s merger boom in France as well as in Britain but it may well be that Brussels is legislating now after the event. As Renaud Gillet, head of Rhône-Poulenc in France says, 'the time of the big acquisitions is over.' His words find echo in the sentiment of many European industrialists nowadays. The idea of merging to emulate the scale of the U.S. multinationals' operations is losing ground. 'Mile long' production lines once seemed to be the thing of the future says Marc Ouin, secretary-general of Renault (speaking figuratively). Now he regards the economies of scale as more trouble than they are worth in human terms.

So, are industrial companies in Europe anxious to merge across national frontiers into the larger units which Brussels holds to be desirable in order to exploit fully the advantages of the EEC? (The irony of the situation is that the Commission seems at the same time to be actively discouraging such mergers through its 'competition' policy though it may be that this aimed mostly at marauding U.S. multi-national companies in Europe). The Fiat Citroën link was rather cynically dissolved when Citroën found that its erstwhile position of weakness (always a good stance from which to concede a merger) had been transformed to one of strength. Franco-Italian commercial rivalry quickly reasserted itself here. The Dunlop-Pirelli union was as John Earle comments, 'hailed at the time as a courageous attempt at European trail blazing and a possible pattern for further links between European companies. In the event, its vicissitudes seem to underline the difficulties rather than the advantages of such mergers.' The answer seems to be that cross frontier mergers can be made to work already in Europe where there is a true need and not just a doctrinal concept behind such an international grouping. The Dutch have demonstrated this with their national genius for international operations through Royal Dutch/Shell and Unilever (both Anglo-Dutch) for instance as well as through ESTEL (Hoogovens-Hoesch) the German-Dutch steel grouping.

Brussels unfortunately seems to flounder whenever it deserts its ivory tower of policy making and come face to face with business reality in Europe. Symptomatic of this was the clash between Signor Altiero Spinelli, the EEC Commissioner for Industry, and Mr Ronald Grierson, then the European Commission's director general for industrial affairs, at the beginning of 1974. Grierson resigned when his essential pragmatism came into head-on conflict with Spinelli's vision of a new industrial order in Europe based on state and supranational intervention. Grierson was being characteristically English and Spinelli characteristically Italian. Neither was being 'European' and indeed if they had been it is highly unlikely that their synthesised view would have corresponded with the diverse reality which is European industry.

Can Brussels persuade companies in the Community of the virtues of greater disclosure of financial information (along British and American lines incidentally)? As this book has shown, some of the most successful companies in Europe, such as Michelin in France or C & A in Holland and a host of others are fiercely reticent about such disclosure. They would probably argue with a great deal of conviction that greater disclosure would divert their attention away from industrial achieve- ment to financial ratios in order to satisfy investment analysts. Some of the leading U.K. companies that have so far avoided selling shares to the public would probably agree with them. It can be argued on the evidence of this survey that, in the main, Continental industry has not suffered through starving its smaller shareholders of information. The banks, holding companies and other controlling institutions have access to the information they need anyway.

Turning to the question of what lessons one EEC country can learn from another's industrial experience there are a number of things which can be usefully learned from this survey, albeit negative ones in some respects.

In Italy where state domination of industry has probably reached the ultimate point in western Europe even the Communist Party is against any extension of the public sector, on the grounds that the state already has enough economic power in its hands to cope with. In Germany even a Social Democrat Government judged it wise to dispose of part of its holding in industry and issued 'People's Shares' in Volkswagen and Preussag for instance. These are points which the British Labour Party no less than the Social Democrat Party in Denmark will do well to bear in mind before proceeding with any major extension of public ownership in their respective countries.

Signor Spinelli recently called for inter-state links between the state-dominated industries of the EEC. Perhaps a more useful exercise for the Commission to undertake would be an examination of the relative performances of industries which are in some cases nationalised in Europe and in others not. Steelmaking and electric power generation are nationalised in Britain though not universally on the Continent while on the other hand parts of the French and German motor industries are Government controlled. In Italy oil exploration is very much the province of the state too as well as in France. Denmark allows three licensed private companies to run much of its telephone service. Subject only to peculiar local conditions, there must be useful lessons to be learned from the operation of such industries in public and private hands.

Britain and Denmark are also flirting with the German concept of *Mitbestimmung* or worker participation in industry. The system, along with its corollary the *Betriebsverfassung* (works council) and two-tier boards ('*Aufsichtsrat*' and '*Vorstand*'), has worked well enough in Germany, or at least industry has learned to live with it. But as Malcolm Rutherford suggests: 'Behind them perhaps is no more than the old German desire for order, which has now been codified.' Oddly, moreover, worker participation in Germany is often subjugated to a high degree of paternalism which management displays towards workers. It is a moot point which is the true unifying factor between the two sides of industry.

Whether *Mitbestimmung* could be transplanted to other countries' industrial systems is open to serious doubt. Likewise it may well be true that the *dirigiste* relationship between French government and industry has worked well there but the French acceptance of *dirigisme* goes back a long way, at least to Napoleon. The Danish Social Democrats' plan to take industry largely out of the hands of existing shareholders and to put it into the hands of the workers failed even to get off the ground there. It may be revived but it is doubtful whether this uniquely Scandinavian concept could ever travel to the Continent or to Britain and survive the journey.

Perhaps the only discernible common trend in European industry is the waning influence of the big private dynasties, though they are still much more strongly entrenched in some countries – Italy for example – than in others. Another area in which a 'European' initiative might be welcome is in examining the rôle and record of these great empires, in sociological as well as economic terms. Alleviating the pressures which so often force their ultimate breakup – fiscal pressures in the main – is after all well within the powers of national administrations if they were flexible enough in their attitude to see fit to do so. The dynasties have, as this book has shown, contributed a good deal to the economic and social stability of Europe and may yet have at least as much to contribute as the 'efficient, grey public corporations' – provided they are given the opportunity.

References

1. D. Robbins & Robert B. Stobaugh, *Money in the Multinational Enterprise*, (Longmans, London 1973). See also: M.A.P. Manser, *Financial Rôle of Multinational Enterprises*, (Cassell & Co., London 1973).
2. Bundesbank Monthly Reports, August 1973 and January 1974.
3. William Manchester, *The Arms of Krupp*, (Michael Joseph, London 1969).
4. This comment appeared in one of the more authoritative articles to appear on the Vatican's finances in recent years, by Paul Horne in the January 1971 issue of the *Institutional Investor*, 488, Madison Avenue, New York.
5. 'Social Capitalism' *Productivity and Amenity*, Croom Helm 1974.
6. M. Briggs and P. Jordan, *Economic History of England* (University Tutorial Press, London 1967).
7. Peter Readman et al, *The European Money Puzzle* p.134 (Michael Joseph, London 1973).
8. Ajit Singh, *Takeovers*, (Cambridge University Press London 1972).
9. Gerald D. Newbould, *Management and Merger Activity*, (Guthstead, London 1970).
10. Christopher Marley, then Financial Editor *The Times*, 2 November 1972.
11. A.J. Merrett and M.E. Lehr, *The Private Company Today* (Gower Press, London 1971).
12. *Sunday Times*, 27 April 1969.
13. Graham Turner, *Business in Britain* (Penguin, London 1971).
14. *Société Générale de Belgique, 1822–1972*, published by the Company on the occasion of its 150th anniversary.
15. Anthony Sampson, *The Sovereign State, the Secret History of ITT* (Hodder and Stoughton, London 1973).
16. Simon Scott Plummer, *The Times*, 15 December 1972.
17. Société Générale de Belgique, Supplement to Bulletin No. 12, March 1973.
18. Giles Merritt, *Financial Times*, 15 September 1972.
19. *Economist*, 18 March 1972.
20. See *Who's Who in Europe* E.A. de Maeyer, published annually by

Europ-Elite, Brussels.

21. *Jane's Major Companies of Europe*, edited by Lionel F. Gray and Jonathon Low; *Jane's Yearbooks* (Sampson Low, Marston & Company, London 1973).

22. David Blake, *Sunday Times*, 16 April 1972.

23. *Morphologie des Groupes Financiers*, Centre de Recherche et d'Information Socio-Politique, Brussels.

24. William Low, *Financial Times*, 12 September 1972.

25. David Cross, *The Times*, 19 July 1972.

26. Frank E. Huggett, *Modern Belgium* (Pall Mall Press, London 1969).

27. Industrial Credit Company, *Focus on Industrial Credit* (Dublin 1969).

28. *Company Taxation in Ireland*, Stationery Office, Dublin.

29. Patrick Lynch and John Vaizey, *Guinness's Brewery in the Irish Economy*, 1759–1876 (Cambridge University Press, London 1960).

30. Annex to the Bills Aiming at Economic Democracy, Ministry of Labour, Copenhagen 1973.

31. Denmark, an Official Handbook, Royal Danish Ministry of Foreign Affairs, Copenhagen (Annually).

INDEX